AN ADDITIONAL NUMBER OF
LETTERS
FROM THE
FEDERAL FARMER
TO THE
REPUBLICAN

LEADING TO A FAIR EXAMINATION OF THE SYSTEM OF GOVERNMENT, PROPOSED BY THE LATE CONVENTION; TO SEVERAL ESSENTIAL AND NECESSARY ALTERATIONS IN IT; AND CALCULATED TO ILLUSTRATE AND SUPPORT THE PRINCIPLES AND POSITIONS LAID DOWN IN THE PRECEDING LETTERS [TOGETHER WITH] OBSERVATIONS ON THE NEW CONSTITUTION, AND ON THE FEDERAL AND STATE CONVENTIONS BY A COLUMBIAN PATRIOT

By Richard Henry Lee

AMERICANA CLASSICS
QUADRANGLE BOOKS, INC.
Chicago

First edition published 1788, New York
This edition published 1962 by
Quadrangle Books, Inc. / Chicago

Library of Congress Catalog Card Number 62-14070

 MANUFACTURED IN THE UNITED STATES OF AMERICA
BOOK CRAFTSMEN ASSOCIATES, INC., NEW YORK

TABLE OF CONTENTS

LETTERS from the FEDERAL FARMER

TO THE

REPUBLICAN.

LETTER VI.

DEAR SIR,

MY former letters to you, refpecting the conftitution propofed, were calculated merely to lead
to a fuller inveftigation of the fubject; having
more extenfively confidered it, and the opinions of
others relative to it, I fhall, in a few letters, more particularly endeavour to point out the defects, and propofe amendments. I fhall in this make only a few
general and introductory obfervations, which, in the
prefent ftate of the momentous queftion, may not be
improper; and I leave you, in all cafes, to decide by a
careful examination of my works, upon the weight of
my arguments, the propriety of my remarks, the up-
rightnefs of my intentions, and the extent of my candor—I prefume I am writing to a man of candor and
reflection, and not to an ardent, peevifh, or impatient
man.

When the conftitution was firft publifhed, there appeared to prevail a mifguided zeal to prevent a fair unbiaffed examination of a fubject of infinite importance
to this people and their pofterity—to the caufe of liberty and the rights of mankind—and it was the duty of
thofe who faw a reftlefs ardor, or defign, attempting
to miflead the people by a parade of names and mif-
reprefentations, to endeavour to prevent their having
their

their intended effects. The only way to stop the passions of men in their career is, coolly to state facts, and deliberately to avow the truth—and to do this we are frequently forced into a painful view of men and measures.

Since I wrote to you in October, I have heard much said, and seen many pieces written, upon the subject in question ; and on carefully examining them on both sides, I find much less reason for changing my sentiments, respecting the good and defective parts of the system proposed than I expected—The opposers, as well as the advocates of it, confirm me in my opinion, that this system affords, all circumstances considered, a better basis to build upon than the confederation. And as to the principal defects, as the smallness of the representation, the insecurity of elections, the undue mixture of powers in the senate, the insecurity of some essential rights, &c. the opposition appears, generally, to agree respecting them, and many of the ablest advocates virtually to admit them—Clear it is, the latter do not attempt manfully to defend these defective parts, but to cover them with a mysterious veil; they concede, they retract ; they say we could do no better : and some of them, when a little out of temper, and hard pushed, use arguments that do more honor to their ingenuity, than to their candor and firmness.

Three states have now adopted the constitution without amendments ; these, and other circumstances, ought to have their weight in deciding the question, whether we will put the system into operation, adopt it, enumerate and recommend the necessary amendments, which afterwards, by three-fourths of the states, may be ingrafted into the system, or whether we will make the amendments prior to the adoption—I only undertake to shew amendments are essential and necessary—how far it is practicable to ingraft them into the plan, prior to the adoption, the state conventions must determine. Our situation is critical, and we have but our choice of evils—We may hazard much by adopting the constitution in its present form—we may hazard more by rejecting it wholly—we may hazard much by long contending about amendments prior to the adoption. The

greatest

greateſt political evils that can befal us, are diſcords and civil wars—the greateſt bleſſings we can wiſh for, are peace, union, and induſtry, under a mild, free, and ſteady government. Amendments recommended will tend to guard and direct the adminiſtration—but there will be danger that the people, after the ſyſtem ſhall be adopted, will become inattentive to amendments—Their attention is now awake—the diſcuſſion of the ſubject, which has already taken place, has had a happy effect—it has called forth the able advocates of liberty, and tends to renew, in the minds of the people, their true republican jealouſy and vigilance, the ſtrongeſt guard againſt the abuſes of power ; but the vigilance of the people is not ſufficiently conſtant to be depended on—Fortunate it is for the body of a people, if they can con‑ tinue attentive to their liberties, long enough to erect for them a temple, and conſtitutional barriers for their permanent ſecurity : when they are well fixed between the powers of the rulers and the rights of the people, they become viſible boundaries, conſtantly ſeen by all, and any tranſgreſſion of them is immediately diſcovered : they ſerve as centinels for the people at all times, and eſpecially in thoſe unavoidable intervals of inattention.

Some of the advocates, I believe, will agree to recom‑ mend *good* amendments ; but ſome of them will only conſent to recommend indefinite, ſpecious, but unim‑ portant ones ; and this only with a view to keep the door open for obtaining, in ſome favourable moment, their main object, a complete conſolidation of the ſtates, and a government much higher toned, leſs republican and free than the one propoſed. If neceſſity, therefore, ſhould ever oblige us to adopt the ſyſtem, and recom‑ mend amendments, the true friends of a federal republic muſt ſee they are well defined, and well calculated, not only to prevent our ſyſtem of government moving fur‑ ther from republican principles and equality, but to bring it back nearer to them—they muſt be conſtantly on their guard againſt the addreſs, flattery, and ma‑ nœuvres of their adverſaries.

The gentlemen who oppoſe the conſtitution, or con‑ tend for amendments in it, are frequently, and with much

much bitterneſs, charged with wantonly attacking the men who framed it. The unjuſtneſs of this charge leads me to make one obſervation upon the conduct of parties, &c. Some of the advocates are only pretended federaliſts ; in fact they wiſh for an abolition of the ſtate governments. Some of them I believe to be honeſt federaliſts, who wiſh to preſerve *ſubſtantially* the ſtate governments united under an efficient federal head ; and many of them are blind tools without any object. Some of the oppoſers alſo are only pretended federaliſts, who want no federal government, or one merely adviſory. Some of them are the true federaliſts, their object, perhaps, more clearly ſeen, is the ſame with that of the honeſt federaliſts ; and ſome of them, probably, have no diſtinct object. We might as well call the advocates and oppoſers tories and whigs, or any thing elſe, as federaliſts and anti-federaliſts. To be for or againſt the conſtitution, as it ſtands, is not much evidence of a federal diſpoſition ; if any names are applicable to the parties, on account of their general politics, they are thoſe of republicans and anti-republicans. The oppoſers are generally men who ſupport the rights of the body of the people, and are properly republicans. The advocates are generally men not very friendly to thoſe rights, and properly anti-republicans.

Had the advocates left the conſtitution, as they ought to have done, to be adopted or rejected on account of its own merits or imperfections, I do not believe the gentlemen who framed it would ever have been even alluded to in the conteſt by the oppoſers. Inſtead of this, the ardent advocates begun by quoting names as inconteſtible authorities for the implicit adoption of the ſyſtem, without any examination—treated all who oppoſed it as friends of anarchy ; and with an indecent virulence addreſſed M—n G—y, L—e, and almoſt every man of weight they could find in the oppſition by name. If they had been candid men they would have applauded the moderation of the oppoſers for not retaliating in this pointed manner, when ſo fair an opportunity was given them ; but the oppoſers generally ſaw that it was no time to heat the paſſions ; but, at the same fame time, they faw there was fomething more than mere zeal in many of their adverfaries ; they faw them attempting to miflead the people, and to precipitate their divifions, by the found of names, and forced to do it, the oppofers, in general terms, alledged thofe names were not of fufficient authority to juftify the hafty adoption of the fyftem contended for. The convention, as a body, was undoubtedly refpectable ; it was, generally, compofed of members of the then and preceding Congreffes : as a body of refpectable men we ought to veiw it. To felect individual names, is an invitation to perfonal attacks, and the advocates, for their own fake, ought to have known the abilities, politics, and fituation of fome of their favourite characters better, before they held them up to view in the manner they did, as men entitled to our implicit political belief : they ought to have known, whether all the men they fo held up to view could, for their paft conduct in public offices, be approved or not by the public records, and the honeft part of the community. Thefe ardent advocates feem now to be peevifh and angry, becaufe, by their own folly, they have led to an invefigation of facts and of political characters, unfavourable to them, which they had not the difcernment to forefee. They may well apprehend they have opened a door to fome Junius, or to fome man, after his manner, with his polite addreffes to men by name, to ftate ferious facts, and unfold the truth ; but thefe advocates may reft affured, that cool men in the oppofition, beft acquainted with the affairs of the country, will not, in the critical paffage of a people from one conftitution to another, purfue inquiries, which, in other circumftances, will be deferving of the higheft praife. I will fay nothing further about political characters, but examine the conftitution ; and as a neceffary and previous meafure to a particular examination, I fhall ftate a few general pofitions and principles, which receive a general affent and briefly notice the leading features of the confederation, and feveral ftate conventions, to which, through the whole invefigation, we muft frequently have recourfe, to aid the mind in its determinations.

B   We

We can put but little dependance on the partial and vague information tranfmitted to us refpecting antient governments; our fituation as a people is peculiar : our people in general have a high fenfe of freedom ; they are high fpirited, though capable of deliberate mea fures ; they are intelligent, difcerning, and well in-formed ; and it is to their condition we muft mould the conftitution and laws. We have no royal or noble fa-milies, and all things concur in favour of a government entirely elective. We have tried our abilities as free-men in a moft arduous conteft, and have fucceeded ; but we now find the main fpring of our movements were the love of liberty, and a temporary ardor, and not any energetic principle in the federal fyftem.

Our territories are far too extenfive for a limited monarchy, in which the reprefentatives muft frequently affemble, and the laws operate mildly and fyftematically. The moft elligible fyftem is a federal republic, that is, a fyftem in which national concerns may be tranfacted in the centre, and local affairs in ftate or diftrict go-vernments.

The powers of the union ought to be extended to commerce, the coin, and national objects ; and a di-vifion of powers, and a depofit of them in different hands, is fafeft.

Good government is generally the refult of experi-ence and gradual improvements, and a punctual execu-tion of the laws is effential to the prefervation of life, liberty, and property. Taxes are always neceffary, and the power to raife them can never be fafely lodged without checks and limitation, but in a full and fub-ftantial reprefentation of the body of the people ; the quantity of power delegated ought to be compenfated by the brevity of the time of holding it, in order to prevent the poffeffors increafing it. The fupreme power is in the people, and rulers poffefs only that portion which is exprefsly given them ; yet the wifeft people have often declared this is the cafe on proper occafions, and have carefully formed ftipulation to fix the extent, and limit the exercife of the power given.

The

The people by Magna Charta, &c. did not acquire powers, or receive privileges from the king, they only ascertained and fixed those they were entitled to as Englishmen ; the title used by the king " we grant," was mere form. Representation, and the jury trial, are the best features of a free government ever as yet discovered, and the only means by which the body of the people can have their proper influence in the affairs of government.

In a federal system we must not only balance the parts of the same government, as that of the state, or that of the union ; but we must find a balancing influence between the general and local governments—the latter is what men or writers have but very little or imperfectly considered.

A free and mild government is that in which no laws can be made without the formal and free consent of the people, or of their constitutional representatives ; that is, of a substantial representative branch. Liberty, in its genuine sense, is security to enjoy the effects of our honest industry and labours, in a free and mild government, and personal security from all illegal restraints.

Of rights, some are natural and unalienable, of which even the people cannot deprive individuals : Some are constitutional or fundamental ; these cannot be altered or abolished by the ordinary laws ; but the people, by express acts, may alter or abolish them—These, such as the trial by jury, the benefits of the writ of habeas corpus, &c. individuals claim under the solemn compacts of the people, as constitutions, or at least under laws so strengthened by long usage as not to be repealable by the ordinary legislature—and some are common or mere legal rights, that is, such as individuals claim under laws which the ordinary legislature may alter or abolish at pleasure.

The confederation is a league of friendship among the states or sovereignties for the common defence and mutual welfare—Each state expresly retains its sovereignty, and all powers not expresly given to congress—All federal powers are lodged in a congress of delegates annually

annually elected by the state legislatures, except in Connecticut and Rhode-Island, where they are chosen by the people—Each state has a vote in congress, pays its delegates, and may instruct or recall them ; no delegate can hold any office of profit, or serve more than three years in any six years—Each state may be represented by not less than two, or more than seven delegates.

Congress (nine states agreeing) may make peace and war, treaties and alliances, grant letters of marque and reprisal, coin money, regulate the alloy and value of the coin, require men and monies of the states by fixed proportions, and appropriate monies, form armies and navies, emit bills of credit, and borrow monies.

Congress (seven states agreeing) may send and receive ambassadors, regulate captures, make rules for governing the army and navy, institute courts for the trial of piracies and felonies committed on the high seas, and for settling territorial disputes between the individual states, regulate weight and measures, post-offices, and Indian affairs.

No state, without the consent of congress, can send or receive embassies, make any agreement with any other state, or a foreign state, keep up any vessels of war or bodies of forces in time of peace, or engage in war, or lay any duties which may interfere with the treaties of congress - Each state must appoint regimental officers, and keep up a well regulated militia—Each state may prohibit the importation or exportation of any species of goods.

The free inhabitants of one state are intitled to the privileges and immunities of the free citizens of the other states—Credit in each state shall be given to the records and judicial proceedings in the others.

Canada, acceding, may be admitted , and any other colony may be admitted by the consent of nine states.

Alterations may be made by the agreement of congress, and confirmation of all the state legislatures.

The following, I think, will be allowed to be unalienable or fundamental rights in the United States :—

No man, demeaning himself peaceably, shall be molested on account of his religion or mode of worship—The

people

people have a right to hold and enjoy their property according to known standing laws, and which cannot be taken from them without their consent, or the consent of their representatives; and whenever taken in the pressing urgencies of government, they are to receive a reasonable compensation for it—Individual security consists in having free recourse to the laws—The people are subject to no laws or taxes not assented to by their representatives constitutionally assembled—They are at all times intitled to the benefits of the writ of habeas corpus, the trial by jury in criminal and civil causes—They have a right, when charged, to a speedy trial in the vicinage : to be heard by themselves or counsel, not to be compelled to furnish evidence against themselves, to have witnesses face to face, and to confront their adversaries before the judge—No man is held to answer a crime charged upon him till it be substantially described to him ; and he is subject to no unreasonable searches or seizures of his person, papers or effects—The people have a right to assemble in an orderly manner, and petition the government for a redress of wrongs —The freedom of the press ought not to be restrained—No emoluments, except for actual service—No hereditary honors, or orders of nobility, ought to be allowed—The military ought to be subordinate to the civil authority, and no soldier be quartered on the citizens without their consent—The militia ought always to be armed and disciplined, and the usual defence of the country—The supreme power is in the people, and power delegated ought to return to them at stated periods, and frequently—The legislative, executive, and judicial powers, ought always to be kept distinct—— others perhaps might be added.

The organization of the state governments—Each state has a legislature, an executive, and a judicial branch—In general legislators are excluded from the important executive and judicial offices—Except in the Carolinas there is no constitutional distinction among Christian sects—The constitutions of New York, Delaware, and Virginia, exclude the clergy from offices civil

C and

and military—the other ſtates do nearly the ſame in
practice.

Each ſtate has a democratic branch elected twice a-
year in Rhode-Iſland and Connecticut, biennially in
South-Carolina, and annually in the other ſtates———
There are about 1500 repreſentatives in all the ſtates,
or one to each 1700 inhabitants, reckoning five blacks
for three whites— he ſtates do not differ as to the age
or moral characters of the electors or elected, nor materially as to their property.

Pennſylvania has lodged all her legiſlative powers in
a ſingle branch. and Georgia has done the ſame; the
other eleven ſtates have each in their legiſlatures a ſecond
or ſenatorial branch. In forming this they have com-
bined various principles, and aimed at ſeveral checks
and balances. It is amazing to ſee how ingenuity has
worked in the ſeveral ſtates to fix a barrier againſt popular inſtability. In Maſſachuſetts the ſenators are
apportioned on diſtricts according to the taxes they
pay, nearly according to property. In Connecticut the
freemen, in September, vote for twenty counſellers, and
return the names of thoſe voted for in the ſeveral towns;
the legiſlature takes the twenty who have the moſt
votes, and give them to the people, who, in April,
chuſe twelve of them, who, with the governor and
deputy governor, form the ſenatorial branch. In Maryland the ſenators are choſen by two electors from each
county; theſe electors are choſen by the freemen, and
qualified as the members in the democratic branch are:
In theſe two caſes checks are aimed at in the mode of
election. Several ſtates have taken into view the periods
of ſervice, age, property, &c. In South-Carolina a
ſenator is elected for two years, in Delaware three, and
in New-York and Virginia four, in Maryland five, and
in the other ſtates for one. In New-York and Virginia
one-fourth part go out yearly. In Virginia a ſenator
muſt be twenty-five years old, in South-Carolina thirty.
In New-York the electors muſt each have a freehold
worth 250 dollars, in North-Carolina a freehold of fifty
acres of land; in the other ſtates the electors of ſenators

tors are qualified as electors of representatives are. In Maffachufetts a fenator muft have a freehold in his own right worth 1000 dollars, or any eftate worth 2000, in New-Jerfey any eftate worth 2666, in South Carolina worth 1300 dollors, in North-Carolina 300 acres of land in fee, &c. The numbers of fenators in each ftate are from ten to thirty-one, about 160 in the eleven ftates, about one to 14000 inhabitants.

Two ftates, Maffachufetts and New-York, have each introduced into their legiflatures a third, but incomplete branch. In the former, the governor may negative any law not fupported by two-thirds of the fenators, and two-thirds of the reprefentatives: in the latter, the governor, chancellor, and judges of the fupreme court may do the fame.

Each ftate has a fingle executive branch. In the five eaftern ftates the people at large elect their governors; in the other ftates the legiflatures elect them. In South Carolina the governor is elected once in two years; in New-York and Delaware once in three, and in the other ftates annually. The governor of New-York has no executive council, the other governors have. In feveral ftates the governor has a vote in the fenatorial branch—the governors have fimilar powers in fome inftances, and quite diffimilar ones in others. The number of executive counfellers in the ftates are from five to twelve. In the four eaftern ftates, New-Jerfey, Pennfylvania, and Georgia, they are of the men returned legiflators by the people. In Pennfylvania the counfellers are chofen triennially, in Delaware every fourth year, in Virginia every three years, in South-Carolina biennially, and in the other ftates yearly.

Each ftate has a judicial branch; each common law courts, fuperior and inferior; fome chancery and admiralty courts: The courts in general fit in different places in order to accommodate the citizens. The trial by jury is had in all the common law courts, and in fome of the admiralty courts. The democratic freemen principally form the juries; men deftitute of property, of character, or under age, are excluded as in elections. Some of the judges are during good behaviour.

C 2   viour.

viour, and fome appointed for a year, and fome for
years ; and all are dependant on the legiflatures for their
falaries—Particulars refpecting this department are too
many to be noticed here.

The FEDERAL FARMER.

L E T T E R   VII.

DECEMBER 31, 1787.

DEAR SIR,

IN viewing the various governments inftituted by
mankind, we fee their whole force reducible to two
principles—the important fprings which alone move the
machines, and give them their intended influence and
controul, are force and perfuafion : by the former men
are compelled, by the latter they are drawn. We de-
nominate a government defpotic or free, as the one or
other principle prevails in it. Perhaps it is not poffible
for a government to be fo defpotic, as not to operate
perfuafively on fome of its fubjects ; nor is it, in the
nature of things, I conceive, for a government to be fo
free, or fo fupported by voluntary confent, as never to
want force to compel obedience to the laws. In defpotic
governments one man, or a few men, independant of the
people, generally make the laws, command obedience,
and inforce it by the fword : one-fourth part of the
people are armed, and obliged to endure the fatigues of
foldiers, to opprefs the others and keep them fubject to
the laws. In free governments the people, or their reprefentatives, make the laws ; their execution is principally the effect of voluntary confent and aid ; the people
refpect the magiftrate, follow their private purfuits, and
enjoy the fruits of their labour with very fmall deductions for the public ufe. The body of the people muft
evidently prefer the latter fpecies of government ; and
it can be only thofe few who may be well paid for the
part they take in enforcing defpotifm, that can, for a
moment,

moment, perfer the former. Our true object is to give full efficacy to one principle, to arm perfuafion on every fide, and to render force as little neceffary as poffible. Perfuafion is never dangerous not even in defpotic governments; but military force, if often applied internally, can never fail to deftroy the love and confidence, and break the fpirits, of the people and to render it totally impracticable and unnatural for him or them who govern, and yield to this force againft the people, to hold their places by the peoples' elections.

I repeat my obfervation, that the plan propofed will have a doubtful operation between the two principles; and whether it will preponderate towards perfuafion or force is uncertain.

Government muft exift—If the perfuafive principle be feeble, force is infallibly the next refort The moment the laws of congrefs fhall be difregarded they muft languifh, and the whole fyftem be convulfed—that moment we muft have recourfe to this next refort, and all freedom vanifh.

It being impracticable for the people to affemble to make laws, they muft elect legiflators, and affign men to the different departments of the government. In the reprefentative branch we muft expect chiefly to collect the confidence of the people, and in it to find almoft entirely the force of perfuafion. In forming this branch, therefore, feveral important confiderations muft be attended to. It muft poffefs abilities to difcern the fituation of the people and of public affairs, a difpofition to fympathize with the people, and a capacity and inclination to make laws congenial to their circumftances and condition : it muft afford fecurity againft interefted combinations, corruption and influence; it muft poffefs the confidence, and have the voluntary fupport of the people.

I think thefe pofitions will not be controverted, nor the one I formerly advanced, that a fair and equal reprefentation is that in which the interefts, feelings, opinions and views of the people are collected, in fuch manner as they would be were the people all affembled. Having made thefe general obfervations, I fhall proceed

to

to confider further my principal pofition, viz. that there is no fubftantial reprefentation of the people provided for in a government, in which the moft effential powers, even as to the internal police of the country, are propofed to be lodged : and to propofe certain amendments as to the reprefentative branch : ıft, That there ought to be *an increafe of the numbers of reprefentatives :* And, 2dly, That the elections of them ought to be better fecured.

1. The reprefentation is unfubftantial and ought to be increafed. In matters where there is much room for opinion you will not expect me to eftablifh my pofitions with mathematical certainty : you muft only expect my obfervations to be candid, and fuch as are well founded in the mind of the writer. I am in a field where doctors difagree ; and as to genuine reprefentation, though no feature in government can be more important, perhaps, no one has been lefs underftood, and no one that has received fo imperfect a confideration by political writers. The ephori in Sparta, and the tribunes in Rome, were but the fhadow : the reprefentation in—Great-Britain is unequal and infecure. In America we have done more in eftablifhing this important branch on its true principles, than, perhaps, all the world befides : yet even here, I conceive, that very great improvements in reprefentation may be made. In fixing this branch, the fituation of the people muft be furveyed, and the number of reprefentatives and forms of election apportioned to that fituation. When we find a numerous people fettled in a fertile and extenfive country, poffeffing equality, and few or none of them oppreffed with riches or wants, it ought to be the anxious care of the conftitution and laws, to arreft them from national depravity, and to preferve them in their happy condition. A virtuous people make juft laws, and good laws tend to preferve unchanged a virtuous people. A virtuous and happy people by laws uncongenial to their characters, may eafily be gradually changed into fervile and depraved creatures. Where the people, or their reprefentatives, make the laws, it is probable they will generally be fitted to the

national

national character and circumftances, unlefs the reprefentation be partial, and the imperfect fubftitute of the
people. However, the people may be electors, if the
reprefentation be fo formed as to give one or more of
the natural claffes of men in the fociety an undue afcen-
dency over the others, it is imperfect ; the former will
gradually become mafters, and the latter flaves It is
the firft of all among the political balances, to preferve
in its proper ftation each of thefe claffes We talk of
balances in the legiflature, and among the departments
of government ; we ought to carry them to the body of
the people. Since I advanced the idea of balancing the
feveral orders of men in a community. in forming a
genuine reprefentation, and feen that idea confidered as
chemerical. I have been fenfibly ftruck with a fentence
in the marquis Beccaria's treatife : this fentence was
quoted by congrefs in 1774, and is as follows :——
" In every fociety there is an effort continually tending
to confer on one part the height of power and happinefs,
and to reduce the others to the extreme of weaknefs and
mifery ; the intent of good laws is to oppofe this effort,
and to diffufe their influence univerfaliy and equally."
Add to this Montefquieu's opinion, that " in a free
ftate every man, who is fuppofed to be a free agent,
ought to be concerned in his own government : therefore, the legiflative fhould refide in the whole body of
the people, or their reprefentatives." It is extremely
clear that thefe writers had in view the feveral orders of
men in fociety, which we call ariftocratical, democratical, merchantile, mechanic, &c. and perceived
the efforts they are conftantly from interefted and ambitious views. difpofed to make to elevate themfelves
and opprefs others. Each order muft have a fhare in
the bufinefs of legiflation actually and efficiently. It is
deceiving a people to tell them they are electors, and
can chufe their legiflators if they cannot, in the nature
of things chufe men from among themfelves, and genuinely like themfelves 1 wifh you to take another
idea along with you ; we are not only to balance thefe
natural efforts, but we are alfo to guard againft accidental combinations ; combinations fouuded in the connections

tions of offices and private interests, both evils which are increased in proportion as the number of men, among which the elected must be, are decreased. To set this matter in a proper point of view, we must form some general ideas and descriptions of the different classes of men, as they may be divided by occupations and politically : the first class is the aristocratical. There are three kinds of aristocracy spoken of in this country—the first is a constitutional one, which does not exist in the United States in our common acceptation of the word. Montesquieu, it is true, observes, that where a part of the persons in a society, for want of property, age, or moral character, are excluded any share in the government, the others, who alone are the constitutional electors and elected, form this aristocracy ; this, according to him, exists in each of the United States, where a considerable number of persons, as all convicted of crimes, under age, or not possessed of certain property, are excluded any share in the government ;—the second is an aristocratic faction ; a junto of unprincipled men, often distinguished for their wealth or abilities, who combine together and make their object their private interests and aggrandizement ; the existence of this description is merely accidental, but particularly to be guarded against. The third is the natural aristocracy ; this term we use to designate a respectable order of men, the line between whom and the natural democracy is in some degree arbitrary ; we may place men on one side of this line, which others may place on the other, and in all disputes between the few and the many, a considerable number are wavering and uncertain themselves on which side they are, or ought to be. In my idea of our natural aristocracy in the United States I include about four or five thousand men ; and among these I reckon those who have been placed in the offices of governors, of members of Congress, and state senators generally, in the principal officers of Congress, of the army and militia, the superior judges the most eminent professional men, &c. and men of large property—the other persons and orders in the community form the natural democracy ; this includes in general
neral

neral the yeomanry, the fubordinate officers, civil and military, the fifhermen, mechanics and traders, many of the merchants and profeffional men. It is eafy to perceive that men of thefe two claffes, the ariftocratical, and democratical, with views equally honeft, have fentiments widely different, efpecially refpecting public and private expences, falaries, taxes, &c. Men of the firft clafs aff'ciate more extenfively, have a high fenfe of honor, poffefs abilities, ambition, and general knowledge; men of the fecond clafs are not fo much ufed to combining great objects; they poff-fs lefs ambition, and a larger fhare of honefty: their dependence is principally on middling and fmall eftates, induftrious purfuits, and hard labour, while that of the former is principally on the emoluments of large eftates, and of the chief offices of government. Not only the efforts of thefe two great parties are to be balanced, but other interefts and parties alfo, which do not always opprefs each other merely for want of power, and for fear of the confequences; though they, in fact, mutually depend on each other: yet fuch are their general views, that the merchants alone would never fail to make laws favourable to themfelves and oppreffive to the farmers, &c the farmers alone would act on like principles; the former would tax the land, the latter the trade. The manufacturers are often difpofed to contend for monopolies, buyers make every exertion to lower prices, and fellers to raife them; men who live by fees and falaries endeavour to raife them, and the part of the people who pay them, endeavour to to lower them; the public creditors to augment the taxes, and the people at large to leffen them. Thus, in every period of fociety, and in all the tranfactions of men, we fee parties verifying the obfervation made by the Marquis; and thofe claffes which have not their centinels in the government, in proportion to what they have to gain or lofe, muft infallibly be ruined.

Efforts among parties are not merely confined to property; they contend for rank and diftinctions; all their paffions in turn are enlifted in political controverfies—Men, elevated in fociety, are often difgufted with the

D   changeablenefs

changeablenefs of the democracy, and the latter are
often agitated with the paffions of jealoufy and envy :
the yeomanry poffefs a large fhare of property and
ftrength. are nervous and firm in their opinions and habits – the mechanics of towns are ardent and changeable,
honeft and credulous. they are inconfiderable for numbers, weight and ftrength, not always fufficiently ftable
for the fupporting free governments : the fifhing intereft partakes partly of the ftrength and ftability of the
landed. and partly of the changeablenefs of the mechanic intereft. As to merchants and traders, they are
our agents in almoft all money tranfactions ; give activity to government, and poffefs a confiderable fhare of
influence in it. It has been obferved by an able writer,
that frugal induftrious merchants are generally advocates
for liberty. It is an obfervation, I believe, well founded, that the fchools produce but few advocates for republican forms of government ; gentlemen of the law,
divinity, phyfic, &c. probably form about a fourth part
of the people ; yet their political influence, perhaps,
is equal to that of all the other defcriptions of men ;
if we may judge from the appointments to Congrefs, the
legal characters will often, in a fmall reprefentation, be
the majority ; but the more the reprefentatives are en-
creafed, the more of the farmers, merchants, &c. will be
found to be brought into the government.

Thefe general obfervations will enable you to difcern
what I intend by different claffes, and the general fcope
of my ideas, when I contend for uniting and balancing
their interefts, feelings, opinions, and views in the legiflature ; we may not only fo unite and balance thefe
as to prevent a change in the government by the gradual exaltation of one part to the depreffion of others,
but we may derive many other advantages from the combination and full reprefentation ; a fmall reprefentation
can never be well informed as to the circumftances of
the people. the members of it muft be too far removed
from the people, in general, to fympathize with them,
and too few to communicate with them : a reprefentation muft be extremely imperfect where the reprefentatives are not circumftanced to make the proper communications

munications to their conftituents, and where the conftituents in turn cannot, with tolerable convenience, make
known their wants, circumftances, and opinions, to
their reprefentatives : where there is but one reprefentative to 30.000 or 40.000 inhabitants, it appears to
me. he can only mix, and be acquainted with a few
refpectable characters among his conftituents, even
double the federal reprefentation, and then there muft
be a very great diftance between the reprefentatives and
the people in general reprefented. On the propofed
plan, the ftate of Delaware, the city of Philadelphia,
the ftate of Rhode Ifland the province of Main, the
county of Suffolk in Maffachufetts will have one reprefentative each ; there can be but little perfonal
knowledge, or but few communications, between him
and the people at large of either of thofe diftricts. It
has been obferved, that mixing only with the refpectable men, he will get the beft information and ideas
from them ; he will alfo receive impreffions favourable
to their purpofes particularly. Many plaufible fhifts
have been made to divert the mind from dwelling on
this defective reprefentation, thefe I fhall confider in
another place.

Could we get over all our difficulties refpecting a balance of interefts and party efforts, to raife fome and
opprefs others, the want of fympathy, information and
intercourfe between the reprefentatives and the people,
an infuperable difficulty will ftill remain, I mean the
conftant liability of a fmall number of reprefentatives
to private combinations ; the tyranny of the one, or
the licentioufnefs of the multitude, are, in my mind,
but fmall evils, compared with the factions of the few.
It is a confideration well worth purfuing, how far this
houfe of reprefentatives will be liable to be formed into
private juntos, how far influenced by expectations of
appointments and offices, how far liable to be managed
by the prefident and fenate, and how far the people
will have confidence in them. To obviate difficulties
on this head, as well as objections to the reprefentative
branch, generally, feveral obfervations have been made—
these

thefe I will now examine, and if they fhall appear to be unfounded, the objections muft ftand unanfwered.

That the people are the electors, muft elect good men, and attend to the adminiftration.

It is faid that the members of Congrefs, at ftated periods, muft return home, and that they muft be fubject to the laws they may make, and to a fhare of the burdens they may impofe.

That the people poffefs the ftrong arm to overawe their rulers, and the beft checks in their national character againft the abufes of power, that the fupreme power will remain in them

That the ftate governments will form a part of, and a balance in the fyftem.

That Congrefs will have only a few national objects to attend to, and the ftate governments many and local ones.

That the new Congrefs will be more numerous than the prefent, and that any numerous body is unwieldy and mobbifh.

That the ftates only are reprefented in the prefent Congrefs, and that the people will require a reprefentation in the new one. that in fifty or an hundred years the reprefentation will be numerous.

That congrefs will have no temptation to do wrong; and that no fyftem to enflave the people is practicable.

That as long as the people are free they will preferve free governments; and that when they fhall become tired of freedom, arbitrary govrnment muft take place.

Thefe obfervations I fhall examine in the courfe of my letters; and, I think, not only fhew that they are not well founded, but point out the fallacy of fome of them; and fhew that others do not very well comport with the dignified and manly fentiments of a free and enlightened people.

THE FEDERAL FARMER.

L E T T E R   VIII.

JANUARY 3, 1788.

DEAR SIR,

BEFORE I proceed to examine the objections, I beg leave to add a valuable idea respecting representation, to be collected from De Lome, and other able writers, which essentially tends to confirm my positions : They very justly impute the establishment of general and equal liberty in England to a balance of interests and powers among the different orders of men ; aided by a series of fortunate events, that never before, and possibly never again will happen.

Before the Norman conquest the people of England enjoyed much of this liberty. The first of the Norman kings, aided by foreign mercenaries and foreign attendants, obnoxious to the English, immediately laid arbitrary taxes, and established arbitrary courts, and severely oppress all orders of people : The barons and people, who recollected their former liberties. were induced, by those oppressions, to unite their efforts in their common defence : Here it became necessary for the great men, instead of deceiving and depressing the people, to enlighten and court them : the royal power was too strongly fixed to be annihilated, and rational means were, therefore directed to limiting it within proper bounds. In this long and arduous task, in this new species of contests, the barons and people succeeded, because they had been freemen, and knew the value of the object they were contending for ; because they were the people of a small island—one people who found it practicable to meet and deliberate in one assembly, and act under one system of resolves, and who were not obliged to meet in different provincial assemblies, as is the case in large countries, as was the case in France, Spain, &c. where their determinations were inconsistent with each other, and where the king could play off one assembly against another.

It was in this united situation the people of England were for several centuries, enabled to combine their exertions,

E   ertions,

ertions, and by compacts, as Magna Charta, a bill of
rights, &c. were able to limit, by degrees, the royal
prerogatives, and eftablifh their own liberties. The
firft combination was, probably, the accidental effect of
pre-exifting circumftances ; but there was an admirable
balance of interefts in it, which has been the parent of
Englifh liberty, and excellent regulations enjoyed fince
that time. The executive power having been uniformly
in the king, and he the vifible head of the nation, it
was chimerical for the greateft lord or moft popular
leader, confiftent with the ftate of the government, and
opinion of the people, to ferioufly think of becoming
the king's rival, or to aim at even a fhare of the executive power ; the greateft fubject's profpect was only in
acquiring a refpectable influence in the houfe of commons, houfe of lords, or in the miniftry ; circumftances
at once made it the interefts of the leaders of the people to ftand by them. Far otherwife was it with the
ephori in Sparta, and tribunes in Rome. The leaders
in England have led the people to freedom, in almoft
all other countries to fervitude. The people in England have made ufe of deliberate exertions, their fafeft
and moft efficient weapons. In other countries they
have often acted like mobs, and been enflaved by their
enemies, or by their own leaders. In England, the
people have been led uniformly, and fyftematically by
their reprefentatives to fecure their rights by compact,
and to abolifh innovations upon the government : they
fucceffively obtained Magna Charta, the powers of
taxation, the power to propofe laws, the habeas corpus act, bill of rights, &c. they, in fhort, fecured general and equal liberty, fecurity to their perfons and
property; and, as an everlafting fecurity and bulwark
of their liberties, they fixed the democratic branch in
the legiflature, and jury trial in the execution of the
laws, the freedom of the prefs, &c.

In Rome, and moft other countries, the reverfe of
all this is true. In Greece, Rome, and wherever the
civil law has been adopted, torture has been admitted.
In Rome the people were fubject to arbitrary confifca-
tions, and even their lives would be arbitrarily difpofed
of

of by confuls, tribunes, dictators, masters, &c. half of
the inhabitants were slaves, and the other half never
knew what equal liberty was; yet in England the people
have had king, lords, and commons; in Rome
they had confuls, senators and tribunes : why then was
the government of England so mild and favourable to
the body of the people, and that of Rome an ambitious and oppressive aristocracy ? Why in England have
the revolutions always ended in stipulations in favour of
general liberty, equal laws, and the common rights of
the people and in most other countries in favour only
of a few influential men ? The reasons, in my mind,
are obvious : In England the people have been substantially represented in many respects ; in the other countries it has not been so. Perhaps a small degree of attention to a few simple facts will illustrate this.—In
England, from the oppressions of the Norman kings
to the revolution in 1688, during which period of two
or three hundred years the English liberties were afcertained and established, the aristocratic part of that
nation was substantially represented by a very large
number of nobles, possessing similar interests and feelings with those they represented. The body of the people, about four or five millions, then mostly a frugal
landed people, were represented by about five hundred
representatives, taken not from the order of men which
formed the aristocracy, but from the body of the people, and possessed of the same interests and feelings.
De Lome, speaking of the British representation, expresly founds all his reasons on this union ; this similitude of interests, feelings, views and circumstances.
He observes, the English have preserved their liberties,
because they and their leaders or representatives have
been strictly united in interests, and in contending for
general liberty. Here we see a genuine balance founded in the actual state of things. The whole community, probably, not more than two-fifths more numerous than we now are, were represented by seven or
eight hundred men ; the barons stipulated with the
common people, and the king with the whole. Had
the legal distinction between lords and commons been

broken

broken down, and the people of that ifland been called upon to·elect forty-five fenators, and one hundred and twenty reprefentatives, about the proportion we propofe to eftablifh, their whole legiflature evidently would have been of the natural ariftocracy, and the body of the people would not have had fcarcely a fingle fincere advocate ; their interefts would have been neglected, general and equal liberty forgot, and the balance loft ; contefts and conciliations, as in moft other countries, would have been merely among the few, and as it might have been neceffary to ferve their purpofes. the people at large·would have been flattered or threatened, and probably not a fingle ftipulation made in their favour.

In Rome the people were miferable, though they had three orders, the confuls, fenators and tribunes, and approved the laws, and all for want of a genuine reprefentation. The people were too numerous to af- femble, and do any thing properly themfelves ; the voice of a few, the dupes of artifice, was called the voice of the people. It is difficult for the people to defend themfelves againft the arts and intrigues of the great, but by felecting a fuitable number of men fixed to their interefts to reprefent them, and to oppofe minifters and fenators. And the people's all depends on the number of the men felected, and the manner of doing it. To be convinced of this, we need only attend to the reafon of the cafe, the conduct of the Britifh commons, and of the Roman tribunes : equal liberty prevails in England, becaufe there was a reprefentation of the people, in fact and reality, to eftablifh it ; equal liberty never prevailed in Rome, becaufe there was but the fhadow of a repre- fentation. There were confuls in Rome annually elected to execute the laws ; feveral hundred fenators repre- fented the great families ; the body of the people an- nually chofe tribunes from among themfelves to defend them and to fecure their rights ; I think the number of tribunes annually chofen never exceeded ten. This re- prefentation, perhaps, was not proportionally fo nu- merous as the reprefentation propofed in the new plan ; but the difference will not appear to be fo great, when it fhall be recollected, that thefe tribunes were chofen annually ;

annually ; that the great patrician families were not admitted to thefe offices of tribunes, and that the people
of Italy who elected the tribunes were a long while, if
not always, a fmall people compared with the people of
the United States. What was the confequence of this
triffling reprefentation ? The people of Rome always
elected for their tribunes men confpicuous for their
riches, military commands, profeffional popularity, &c.
great commoners, between whom and the noble families
there was only the fhadowy difference of legal diftinction. Among all the tribunes the people chofe for feveral centuries, they had fcarcely five real friends to
their interefts. Thefe tribunes lived, felt and faw, not
like the people, but like the great patrician families,
like fenators and great officers of ftate, to get into
which it was evident, by their conduct, was their fole object. Thefe tribunes often talked about the rights and
prerogatives of the people, and that was all ; for they
never even attempted to eftablifh equal liberty : fo far
from eftablifhing the rights of the people, they fuffered
the fenate, to the exclufion of the people, to engrofs
the powers of taxation ; thofe excellent and almoft only
real weapons of defence even the people of England poffefs. The tribunes obtained that the people fhould be
eligible to fome of the great offices of ftate, and marry,
if they pleafed, into the noble families ; thefe were advantages in their nature, confined to a few elevated
commoners, and of triffling importance to the people
at large. Nearly the fame obfervations may be made as
to the ephori of Sparta.

We may amufe ourfelves with names ; but the fact is,
men will be governed by the motives and temptations
that furround their fituation. Political evils to be
guarded againft are in the human character, and not in
the name of patrician or plebian. Had the people of
Italy, in the early period of the republic, felected yearly, or biennially, four or five hundred of their beft informed men, emphatically from among themfelves,
thefe reprefentatives would have formed an honeft refpectable affembly, capable of combining in them the
views and exertions of the people, and their refpectability,

lity would have procured them honeft and able leaders, and we fhould have feen equal liberty eftablifhed. True liberty ftands in need of a foftering hand ; from the days of Adam fhe has found but one temple to dwell in fecurely ; fhe has laid the foundation of one, perhaps her laft. in America ; whether this is to be compleated and have duration, is yet a queftion. Equal liberty never yet found many advocates among the great : it is a difagreeable truth, that power perverts mens views in a greater degree, than public employments inform their underftandings -- they become hardened in certain maxims, and more loft to fellow feelings. Men may always be too cautious to commit alarming and glaring iniquities ; but they, as well as fyftems, are liable to be corrupted by flow degrees. Junius well obferves, we are not only to guard againft what men will do, but even againft what they may do. Men in high public offices are in ftations where they gradually lofe fight of the people, and do not often think of attending to them, except when neceffary to anfwer private purpofes.

The body of the people muft have this true reprefentative fecurity placed fome where in the nation ; and in the United States, or in any extended empire, I am fully perfuaded can be placed no where, but in the forms of a federal republic, where we can divide and place it in feveral ftate or diftrict legiflatures, giving the people in thefe the means of oppofing heavy internal taxes and oppreffive meafures in the proper ftages. A great empire contains the amities and animofities of a world within itfelf. We are not like the people of England, one people compactly fettled on a fmall ifland, with a great city filled with frugal merchants, ferving as a common centre of liberty and union : we are difperfed, and it is impracticable for any but the few to affemble in one place : the few muft be watched, checked, and often refifted—tyranny has ever fhewn a prediliction to be in clofe amity with them, or the one man. Drive it from kings and it flies to fenators, to dicemvirs, to dictators, to tribunes, to popular leaders, to military chiefs, &c.

De

De Lome well obferves, that in focieties, laws which were to be equal to all are foon warped to the private interefts of the adminiftrators, and made to defend the ufurpations of a few. The Englifh, who had tafted the fweets of equal laws, were aware of this, and though they reftored their king, they carefully delegated to parliament the advocates of freedom.

I have often lately heard it obferved, that it will do very well for a people to make a conftitution, and ordain, that at ftated periods they will chufe, in a certain manner, a firft magiftrate, a given number of fenators and reprefentatives, and let them have all power to do as they pleafe. This doctrine, however it may do for a fmall republic, as Connecticut, for inftance, where the people may chufe fo many fenators and reprefentatives to affemble in the legiflature, in an eminent degree, the interefts, the views, feelings, and genuine fentiments of the people themfelves, can never be admitted in an extenfive country; and when this power is lodged in the hands of a few, not to limit the few, is but one ftep fhort of giving abfolute power to one man—in a numerous reprefentation the abufe of power is a common injury, and has no temptation—among the few, the abufe of power may often operate to the private emolument of thofe who abufe it.

THE FEDERAL FARMER.

LETTER IX.

JANUARY 4, 1788.

DEAR SIR,

THE advocates of the conftitution fay we muft truft to the adminiftration, and elect good men for reprefentatives I admit, that in forming the focial compact, we can fix only general principles, and, of neceffity, muft truft fomething to the wifdom and integrity of the adminiftration. But the queftion is, do we not truft too much, and to men alfo placed in the

vortex

vortex of temptation, to lay hold of proffered advantages for themselves and their connections, and to opprefs the body of the people.

It is one thing to authorife a well organized legifla-ture to make laws, under the reftraints of a well guarded conftitution, and another to affemble a few men, and to tell them to do what they pleafe. I am not the more fhaken in my principles, or difpofed to defpair of the caufe of liberty, becaufe fome of our able men have adopted the yielding language of non-refiftance, and writers dare infult the people with the fignatures of Cæfar, Mark Antony, and of other tyrants ; becaufe I fee even moderate and amiable men, forced to let go of monarchy in 1775, ftill in love with it, to ufe the fimile of our countrymen, when the political pot boils, the fkum will often get uppermoft and make its appear-ance. I believe the people of America, when they fhall fully underftand any political fubject brought be-fore them, will talk in a very different ftile, and ufe the manly language of freedom.

But " the people muft elect good men :"—Examine the fyftem, Is it practicable for them to elect fit and proper reprefentatives where the number is fo fmall ? " But the people may chufe whom they pleafe." This is an obfervation, I believe, made without due attention to facts and the ftate of the community. To explain my meaning, I will confider the defcriptions of men com-monly prefented to the people as candidates for the offices of reprefentatives—we may rank them in three claffes : 1. The men who form the natural ariftocracy, as before defined. 2. Popular demagogues : thefe men alfo are often politically elevated, fo as to be feen by the people through the extent of large diftricts ; they often have fome abilities, without principle, and rife into notice by their noife and arts. 3. The fubftantial and refpectable part of the democracy , they are a nu-merous and valuable fet of men, who difcern and judge well. but from being generally filent in public affemblies are often overlooked : they are the moft fubftantial and beft informed men in the feveral towns, who occafionally fill the middle grades of offices, &c. who hold not a

fpendid

splendid, but a respectable rank in private concerns: these men are extensively diffused through all the counties, towns and small districts in the union ; even they, and their immediate connections, are raised above the majority of the people. and as representatives are only brought to a level with a more numerous part of the community, the middle orders, and a degree nearer the mass of the people. Hence it is that the best practical representation, even in a small state, must be several degrees more aristocratical than the body of the people. A representation so formed as to admit but few or none of the third class, is, in my opinion, not deserving of the name--even in armies, courts-martial are so formed as to admit subaltern officers into them. The true idea is, so to open and enlarge the representation as to let in a due proportion of the third class with those of the first. Now, my opinion is, that the representation proposed is so small as that ordinarily very few or none of them can be elected ; and, therefore, after all the parade of words and forms the government must possess the soul of aristocracy, or something worse, the spirit of popular leaders.

I observed in a former letter, that the state of Delaware of Rhode-Island the Province of Main, and each of the great counties in Massachusetts &c would have one member, and rather more than one when the representatives shall be increased to one for each 30.000 inhabitants In some districts the people are more dispersed-and unequal than in others : In Delaware they are compact, in the Province of Main dispersed ; how can the elections in either of those districts be regulated so as that a man of the third class can be elected ?— Exactly the same principles and motives, the same uncontroulable circumstances, must govern the elections as in the choice of the governors. Call upon the people of either of those districts to chuse a governor, and it will, probably, never happen that they will not bestow a major part, or the greatest number, of their votes on some very conspicuous or very popular character. A man that is known among a few thousands of people, may be quite unknown among thirty or forty thousand.

F

On

On the whole, it appears to me to be almoſt a ſelf-evident
poſition, that when we call on thirty or forty thouſand
inhabitants to unite in giving their votes for one man, it
will be uniformly impracticable for them to unite in
any men, except thoſe few who have became eminent for
their civil or military rank, or their popular legal abilities : it will be found totally impracticable for men in
the private walks of life, except in the profeſſion of the
law, to become conſpicuous enough to attract the notice of ſo many electors and have their ſuffrages.

But if I am right, it is aſked why ſo many reſpectable men advocate the adoption of the propoſed ſyſtem. Several reaſons may be given — many of our gentlemen are attached to the principles of monarchy and
ariſtocracy ; they have an averſion to democratic republics. The body of the people have acquired large
powers and ſubſtantial influence by the revolution. In
the unſettled ſtate of things, their numerous repreſentatives, in ſome inſtances, miſuſed their powers and
have induced many good men ſuddenly to adopt ideas
unfavourable to ſuch republics, and which ideas they
will diſcard on reflection. Without ſcrutinizing into
the particulars of the propoſed ſyſtem, we immediately
perceive that its general tendency is to collect the powers of government, now in the body of the people in
reality, and to place them in the higher orders and
fewer hands ; no wonder then that all thoſe of and
about theſe orders are attached to it ; they feel there is
ſomething in this ſyſtem advantageous to them. On the
other hand, the body of the people evidently feel there
is ſomething wrong and diſadvantageous to them ; both
deſcriptions perceive there is ſomething tending to be-
ſtow on the former the height of power and happineſs,
and to reduce the latter to weakneſs, inſignificance,
and miſery. The people evidently feel all this though
they want expreſſions to convey their ideas. Further,
even the reſpectable part of the democracy, have never
yet been able to diſtinguiſh clearly where the fallacy
lies ; they find there are defects in the confederation ;
they ſee a ſyſtem preſented, they think ſomething muſt
be done ; and, while their minds are in ſuſpence, the
zealous

zealous advocates force a reluctant confent. Nothing
can be a ftronger evidence of the nature of this fyftem,
than the general fenfe of the feveral orders in the community refpecting its tendency the parts taken generally by them proves my pofition, that notwithftanding
the parade of words and forms, the government muft
poffefs the foul of ariftocracy.

Congrefs, heretofore, have afked for moderate additional powers, the cry was give them—be federal but the
proper diftinction between the cafes that produce this
difpofition, and the fyftem propofed, has not been fairly made and feen in all its confequences. We have feen
fome of our ftate reprefentations too numerous and
without examining a medium we run into the oppofite
extreme. It is true, the proper number of federal reprefentatives, is matter of opinion in fome degree : but
there are extremes which we immediately perceive, and
others, which we clearly difcover on examination We
fhould readily pronounce a reprefentative branch of 15
members fmall in a federal government, having complete powers as to taxes, military matters, commerce,
the coin, &c &c On the other hand, we fhould readily
pronounce a federal reprefentation as numerous as thofe
of the feveral ftates confifting of about 1500 reprefentatives, unwieldly and totally improper. It is afked,
has not the wifdom of the convention found the medium ? perhaps not : The convention was divided on
this point of numbers : at leaft fome of its ableft members urged, that inftead of 65 reprefentatives there
ought to be 130 in the firft inftance : They fixed one
reprefentative for each 40 000 inhabitants, and at the
clofe of the work, the prefident fuggefted, that the
reprefentation appeared to be too fmall and without debate, it was put at, not exceeding one for each 30,000.
I mention thefe facts to fhew, that the convention went
on no fixed data. In this extenfive country it is difficult to get a reprefentation fufficiently numerous : Neceffity, I believe, will oblige us to facrifice in fome degree the true genuine principles of reprefentation. But
this facrifice ought to be as little as poffible : How far
we ought to increafe the reprefentation I will not pretend

tend to fay ; but that we ought to increafe it very confiderably, is clear—to double it t leaft, making full
allowances for the ftate reprefentations : and this we
may evidently do and approach accordingly towards
fafety and perfection without ncountering any incon-
veniences   It is with great difficulty the people can
unite thefe different interefts and views even tolerably,
in the ftate fenators, who are more than twice as numerous as the federal reprefentatives, as propofed by the
convention ; even thefe fenators are confidered as fo far
removed from the people. that they are not allowed
immediately to hold their purfe ftrings

The principle objections made to the increafe of the
reprefentation are, the expence and difficulty in getting
the members to attend.   The fi ft cannot be important;
the laft if founded. is againft any federal government.
As to the expence, I prefume, the houfe of reprefentatives will not be in feffions more than four months in the
year.   We find by experience. that about two-thirds of
the members of reprefentative affemblies ufually attend ;
therefore, of the reprefentation propofed by the convention, about forty five members probably will attend,
doubling their number. about 90 will probably attend :
their pay, in one cafe, at four dollars a day each (which
is putting it high enough) will amount to, yearly,
21 600 dollars ; in the other cafe, 43 200 dollars difference 21,600 dollars ;—reduce the ftate reprefentatives
from 1500 down to 1000, and thereby fave the atten-
dan e of two thirds of the 500, fay three months in a
year at one dollar and a quarter a day each 3 125
dollars thus we may leave the ftate reprefentations
fufficient large. and yet fave enough by the reduction
nearly to fupport exceeding well the whole federal reprefentation I propofe Surely we never can be fo unwife as to facrifice, effentially, the all-important principles of reprefentation for fo fmall a fum as 21,600
dollars a year for the United States ; a fingle company
of foldiers would coft this fum. It is a fact that can
eafily be fhewn, that we expend three times this fum
every year upon ufelefs inferior offices and very trifling
concerns. It is alfo a fact which can be fhewn, that the
United

United States in the late war fuffered more by a faction
in the federal government, than the pay of the federal
reprefentation will amount to for twenty years.

As to the attendance—Can we be fo unwife as to eftablifh an unfafe and inadequate reprefentative branch, and
give it asa reafon, that we believe only a few members will
be induced to attend ; we ought certainly to eftablifh
an adequate reprefentative branch, and adopt meafures
to induce an attendance ; I believe that a due proportion of 130 or 140 members may be induced to attend :
there are various reafons for the non-attendance of the
members of the prefent congrefs ; it is to be prefumed
that thefe will not exift under the new fyftem.

To compenfate for the want of a genuine reprefentation in a government, where the purfe and fword, and
all important powers, are propofed to be lodged, a
variety of unimportant things are enumerated by the
advocates of it.

In the fecond place, it is faid the members of congrefs muft return home, and fhare in the burdens they
may impofe; and, therefore, private motives will induce
them to make mild laws, to fupport liberty, and eafe
the burdens of the people : this brings us to a mere
queftion of intereft under this head. I think thefe
obfervations will appear, on examination, altogether
fallacious ; becaufe this individual intereft, which may
coincide with the rights and interefts of the people, will
be far more than balanced by oppofite motives and
oppofite interefts. If, on a fair calculation, a man will
gain more by meafures oppreffive to others than he will
lofe by them, he is interefted in their adoption. It is
true, that thofe who govern, generally, by increafing
the public burdens increafe their own fhare of them ?
but by this increafe they may, and often do, increafe
their falaries, fees, and emoluments, in a ten-fold proportion, by increafing falaries, forming armies and
navies, and by making offices—If it fhall appear the
members of congrefs will have thefe temptations before
them, the argument is on my fide—they will view the
account, and be induced continually to make efforts

G   advantageous

advantageous to themfelves and connections, and oppreffive to others.

We muft examine facts—Congrefs, in its prefent
form, have but few offices to difpofe of worth the attention of the members, or of men of the ariftocracy ;
yet, from 1774 to this time, we find a large proportion
of thofe offices affigned to thofe who were or had been
members of congrefs, and though the ftates chufe annually fixty or feventy members, many of them have
been provided for : but few men are known to congrefs in this extenfive country, and, probably, but few
will be to the prefident and fenate, except thofe who
have or fhall appear as members of congrefs, or thofe
whom the members may bring forward. The ftates
may now chufe yearly ninety-one members of congrefs ;
under the new conftitution they will have it in their
power to chufe exactly the fame number, perhaps
afterwards, one hundred and fifteen, but thefe muft be
chofen once in two and fix years ; fo that, in the courfe
of ten years together, not more than two-thirds fo many
members of congrefs will be elected and brought into
view, as there now are under the confederation in the
fame term of time : but at leaft there will be five, if not
ten times, as many offices and places worthy the attention of the members, under the new conftitution, as
there are under the confederation : therefore, we may
fairly prefume, that a very great proportion of the
members of congrefs, efpecially the influential ones,
inftead of returning to private life, will be provided for
with lucrative offices, in the civil or military department,
and not only the members, but many of their fons,
friends, and connection. Thefe offices will be in the
conftitutional difpofition of the prefident and fenate,
and, corruption out of the queftion, what kind of fecurity
can we expect in a reprefentation, fo many of the members of which may rationally feel themfelves candidates
for thefe offices ?—let common fenfe decide. It is true,
that members chofen to offices muft leave their feats in
congrefs, and to fome few offices they cannot be elected
till the time fhall be expired for which they were elected
members ;

members; but this scarcely will effect the bias arising
from the hopes and expectations of office.

It is not only in this point of view, the members of
congress, by their efforts, may make themselves and
friends powerful and happy, while the people may be
oppressed : but there is another way in which they may
soon warp laws, which ought to be equal, to their own
advantages, by those imperceptible means, and on those
doubtful principles which may not alarm. No society
can do without taxes; they are the efficient means of
safety and defence, and they too have often been the
weapons by which the blessings of society have been
destroyed. Congress will have power to lay taxes at
pleasure for the general welfare ; and if they mis-judge
of the general welfare, and lay unnecessary oppressive
taxes, the constitution will provide, as I shall hereafter
shew, no remedy for the people or states—the people
must bear them, or have recourse, not to any constitutional checks or remedies, but to that resistence which
is the last resort, and founded in self-defence.

It is well stipulated, that all duties, imposts, and
excises shall be equal ; and that direct taxes shall be
apportioned on the several states by a fixed rule, but
nothing further. Here commences a dangerous power
in matters of taxation, lodged without any regard to
the balance of interests of the different orders of men,
and without any regard to the internal policy of the
states. Congress having assigned to any state its quota,
say to New-Jersey, 80,000 dollars in a given tax, congress will be entirely at liberty to apportion that sum
on the counties and towns, polls, lands, houses, labour,
&c. and appoint the assessors and collectors in that state
in what manner they please ; there will be nothing to
prevent a system of tax laws being made, unduly to ease
some descriptions of men and burden others ; though
such a system may be unjust and injudicious, though we
may complain, the answer will be, congress have the
power delegated by the people, and, probably, congress
has done what it thought best.

By the confederation taxes must be quotaed on the several states by fixed rules, as before mentioned : but then

each

each ftate's quota is apportioned on the feveral numbers and claffes of citizens in the ftate, by the ftate legiflature, affeffed and collected by ftate laws. Great pains have been taken to counfound the two cafes, which are as diftinct as light and darknefs; this I fhall endeavour to illuftrate, when I come to the amendment refpecting internal taxes. I fhall only obferve, at prefent, that in the ftate legiflatures the body of the people will be genuinely reprefented, and in congrefs not; that the right of refifting oppreffive meafures is inherent in the people, and that a conftitutional barrier fhould be fo formed, that their genuine reprefentatives may ftop an oppreffive ruinous meafure in its early progrefs, before it fhall come to maturity, and the evils of it become in a degree fixed.

It has lately been often obferved, that the power or body of men intrufted with the national defence and tranquility, muft neceffarily poffefs the purfe unlimitedly, that the purfe and fword muft go together—this is new doctrine in a free country, and by no means tenable. In the Britifh government the king is particularly intrufted with the national honor and defence, but the commons folely hold the purfe. I think I have amply fhewn that the reprefentation in congrefs will be totally inadequate in matters of taxation, &c. and, therefore, that the ultimate controul over the purfe muft be lodged elfewhere.

We are not to expect even honeft men rigidly to adhere to the line of ftrict impartiality, where the intereft of themfelves or friends is particularly concerned; if we do expect it, we fhall deceive ourfelves, and make a wrong eftimate of human nature.

But it is afked how fhall we remedy the evil, fo as to complete and perpetuate the temple of equal laws and equal liberty? Perhaps we never can do it. Poffibly we never may be able to do it in this immenfe country, under any one fyftem of laws however modified; neverthelefs, at prefent, I think the experiment worth a making. I feel an averfion to the difunion of the ftates, and to feparate confederacies; the ftates have fought and bled in a common caufe, and great dangers too may attend thefe confederacies. I think the fyftem propofed

capable

capable of very confiderable degrees of perfection, if
we purfue firft principles. I do not think that De
Lome, or any writer I have feen, has fufficiently purfued the proper inquiries and efficient means for making
reprefentation and balances in government more perfect;
it is our tafk to do this in America. Our object is
equal liberty, and equal laws diffufing their influence
among all orders of men ; to obtain this we muft guard
againft the biafs of intereft and paffions, againft interefted combinations, fecret or open; we muft aim at a
balance of efforts and ftrength.

Clear it is, by increafing the reprefentation we leffen
the profpects of each member of congrefs being provided for in public offices ; we proportionably leffen
official influence, and ftrengthen his profpects of becoming a private citizen, fubject to the common burdens,
without the compenfation of the emoluments of office.
By increafing the reprefentation we make it more difficult to corrupt and influence the members ; we diffufe
them more extenfively among the body of the people,
perfect the balance, multiply information, ftrengthen
the confidence of the people, and confequently fupport
the laws on equal and free principles. There are two
other ways, I think, of obtaining in fome degree the
fecurity we want ; the one is, by excluding more extenfively the members from being appointed to offices ;
the other is, by limiting fome of their powers ; but
thefe two I fhall examine hereafter.

THE FEDERAL FARMER.

LETTER

LETTER X.

DEAR SIR,

IT is said that our people have a high sense of freedom, possess power, property, and the strong arm;
meaning, I presume, that the body of the people can
take care of themselves, and awe their rulers; and,
therefore, particular provision in the constitution for
their security may not be essential. When I come to examine these observations, they appear to me too triffling
and loose to deserve a serious answer.

To palliate for the smallness of the representation,
it is observed, that the state governments in which the
people are fully represented, necessarily form a part of
the system. This idea ought to be fully examined.
We ought to enquire if the convention have made the
proper use of these essential parts; the state governments
then we are told will stand between the arbitrary exercise of power and the people: true they may, but armless and helpless, perhaps, with the privilege of making
a noise when hurt—this is no more than individuals
may do. Does the constitution provide a single check
for a single measure, by which the state governments
can constitutionally and regularly check the arbitrary
measures of congress? Congress may raise immediately
fifty thousand men, and twenty millions of dollars in
taxes, build a navy, model the militia, &c. and all
this constitutionally. Congress may arm on every point,
and the state governments can do no more than an individual, by petition to congress, suggest their measures
are alarming and not right.

I conceive the position to be undeniable, that the
federal government will be principally in the hands of
the natural aristocracy, and the state governments principally in the hands of the democracy, the representatives of the body of the people. These representatives
in Great-Britain hold the purse, and have a negative
upon all laws. We must yield to circumstances, and
depart something from this plan, and strike out a new
                                        medium

medium, fo as to give efficacy to the whole fyftem, fup-
ply the wants of the union, and leave the feveral ftates,
or the people affembled in the ftate legiflatures, the
means of defence.

It has been often mentioned, that the objects of
congrefs will be few and national, and require a fmall
reprefentation ; that the objects of each ftate will be
many and local, and require a numerous reprefentation.
This circumftance has not the weight of a feather in my
mind. It is certainly unadvifable to lodge in 65 reprefentatives, and 26 fenators, unlimited power to eftablifh
fyftems of taxation, armies, navies, model the militia,
and to do every thing that may effentially tend foon to
change, totally, the affairs of the community and to
affemble 1500 ftate reprefentatives, and 160 fenators, to
make fence laws, and laws to regulate the defcent and
conveyance of property, the adminiftration of juftice
between man and man, to appoint militia officers, &c.

It is not merely the quantity of information I contend for. Two taxing powers may be inconvenient ;
but the point is, congrefs, like the fenate of Rome,
will have taxing powers, and the people no check——
when the power is abufed, the people may complain
and grow angry, fo may the ftate governments ; they
may remonftrate and counteract, by paffing laws to
prohibit the collection of congreffional taxes ; but
thefe will be acts of the people, acts of fovereign power,
the denier refort unknown to the conftitution ; acts operating in terrorum, acts of refiftence, and not the exercife of any conftitutional power to ftop or check a
meafure before matured : a check properly is the ftop-
ping, by one branch in the fame legiflature, a meafure
propofed by the other in it. In fact the conftitution
provides for the ftates no check, properly fpeaking,
upon the meafures of congrefs—Congrefs can immediately enlift foldiers, and apply to the pockets of the
people.

Thefe few confiderations bring us to the very ftrong
diftinction between the plan that operates on federal
principles, and the plan that operates on confolidated
principles. A plan may be federal or not as to its
organization ;

organization; each state may retain its vote or not; the sovereignty of the state may be represented, or the people of it. A plan may be federal or not as to its operations—federal when it requires men and monies of the states, and the states as such make the laws for raising the men and monies—Not federal, when it leaves the states governments out of the question, and operates immediately upon the persons and property of the citizens. The first is the case with the confederation, the second with the new plan: in the first the state governments may be check, in the last none at all. This distinction I shall pursue further hereafter, under the head before mentioned, of amendments as to internal taxes. And here I shall pursue a species of checks which writers have not often noticed.

To excuse the smallness of the representation, it is said the new congress will be more numerous than the old one. This is not true; and for the facts I refer you to my letter of the 4th instant, to the plan and confederation besides there is no kind of similitude between the two plans. The confederation is a mere league of the states, and congress is formed with the particular checks, and possess the united powers, enumerated in my letter of the 25th ult. The new plan is totally a different thing: a national government to many purposes administered, by men chosen for two, four, and six years, not re-callable, and among whom there will be no rotation; operating immediately in all money and military matters, &c. on the persons and property of the citizens — I think, therefore, that no part of the confederation ought to be adduced for supporting or injuring the new constitution. It is also said that the constitution gives no more power to congress than the confederation, respecting money and military matters; that congress, under the confederation, may require men and monies to any amount, and the states are bound to comply. This is generally true; but, I think, I shall in a subsequent letter satisfactorily prove, that the states have well founded checks for securing their liberties.

I admit the force of the observation, that all the federal powers, by the confederation, are lodged in a
single

fingle affembly ; however, I think much more may be faid in defence of the leading principles of the confederation. I do not object to the qualifications of the electors of reprefentatives, and I fully agree that the people ought to elect one branch.

Further, it may be obferved, that the prefent congrefs is principally an executive body, which ought not to be numerous ; that the houfe of reprefentatives will be a mere legiflative branch, and being the democratic one, ought to be numerous. It is one of the greateft advantages of a government of different branches, that each branch may be conveniently made conformable to the nature of the bufinefs affigned it, and all be made conformable to the condition of the feveral orders of the people. After all the poffible checks and limitations we can devife, the powers of the union muft be very extenfive ; the fovereignty of the nation cannot produce the object in view, the defence and tranquility of the whole, without fuch powers, executive and judicial. I diflike the prefent congrefs a fingle, affembly, becaufe it is impoffible to fit it to receive thofe powers : the executive and judicial powers, in the nature of things, ought to be lodged in a few hands, the legiflature in many hands ; therefore want of fafety, and unavoidable hafty meafures, out of the queftion, they never can all be lodged in one affembly properly — it, in its very formation, muft imply a contradiction.

In objection to increafing the reprefentation, it has alfo been obferved, that it is difficult to affemble a hundred men or more without making them tumultuous and a mere mob ; reafon and experience do not fupport this obfervation. The moft refpectable affemblies we have any knowledge of and the wifeft, have been thofe, each of which confifted of feveral hundred members ; as the fenate of Rome, of Carthage, of Venice, the Britifh Parliament, &c. &c. I think I may without hazarding much, affirm, that our more numerous ftate affemblies and conventions have univerfally difcovered more wifdom, and as much order, as the lefs numerous ones : There muft be alfo a very great difference between the characters of two or three hundred men affembled from

H

a single state, and the characters of the number or half the number assembled from all the united states.

It is added, that on the proposed plan the house of representatives in fifty or a hundred years, will consist of several hundred members : The plan will begin with sixty-five, and we have no certainty that the number ever will be encreased, for this plain reason—that all that combination of interests and influence which has produced this plan, and supported so far, will constantly oppose the increase of the representation, knowing that thereby the government will become more free and democratic : But admitting, after a few years, there will be a member for each 30,000 inhabitants, the observation is trifling, the government is in a considerable measure to take its tone from its early movements, and by means of a small representation it may in half of 50 or 100 years, get moved from its basis, or at least so far as to be incapable of ever being recovered. We ought, therefore, on every principle now to fix the government on proper principles, and fit to our present condition— when the representation shall become too numerous, alter it ; or we may now make provision, that when the representation shall be increased to a given number, that then there shall be one for each given number of inhabitants, &c.

Another observation is, that congress will have no temptations to do wrong—the men that make it must be very uninformed, or suppose they are talking to children. In the first place, the members will be governed by all those motives which govern the conduct of men, and have before them all the allurements of offices and temptations, to establish unequal burdens, before described. In the second place, they and their friends, probably, will find it for their interests to keep up large armies, navies, salaries, &c. and in laying adequate taxes. In the third place, we have no good grounds to presume, from reason or experience, that it will be agreeable to their characters or views, that the body of the people should continue to have power effectually to interfere in the affairs of government. But it is confidently added, that congress will not have it in their
power

power to oppress or enslave the people, that the people will not bear it. It is not supposed that congress will act the tyrant immediately, and in the face of day light. It is not supposed congress will adopt important mea-sures, without plausible pretences, especially those which may tend to alarm or produce opposition. We are to consider the natural progress of things : that men unfriendly to republican equality will go systematically to work, gradually to exclude the body of the people from any share in the government, first of the substance, and then of the forms. The men who will have these views will not be without their agents and supporters. When we reflect, that a few years ago we established democratic republics, and fixed the state governments as the barriers between congress and the pockets of the people ; what great progress has been made in less than seven years to break down those barriers, and essentially to change the principles of our governments, even by the armless few : is it chimerical to suppose that in fif-teen or twenty years to come, that much more can be performed, especially after the adoption of the con-stitution, when the few will be so much better armed with power and influence, to continue the struggle ? probably, they will be wise enough never to alarm, but gradually prepare the minds of the people for one spe-cious change after another, till the final object shall be obtained. Say the advocates, these are only possibi-lities—they are probabilities, a wise people ought to guard against ; and the address made use of to keep the evils out of sight, and the means to prevent them, con-firm my opinion.

But to obviate all objections to the proposed plan in the last resort : it is said our people will be free, so long as they possess the habits of freemen, and when they lose them, they must receive some other forms of government. To this I shall only observe, that this is very humiliating language, and can, I trust, never suit a manly people, who have contended nobly for liberty, and declared to the world they will be free.

I have dwelt much longer than I expected upon the increasing the representation, the democratic interest in the

the federal fyftem ; but I hope the importance of the fubject will juftify my dwelling upon it. I have purfued it in a manner new, and I have found it neceffary to be fomewhat prolix, to illuftrate the point I had in view. My idea has ever been, when the democratic branch is weak and fmall, the body of the people have no defence, and every thing to fear ; if they expect to find genuine political friends in kings and nobles, in great and powerful men, they deceive themfelves. On the other hand, fix a genuine democratic branch in the government, folely to hold the purfe, and with the power of impeachment, and to propofe and negative laws, cautioufly limit the king and nobles, or the executive and the fenate, as the cafe may be, and the people, I conceive, have but little to fear, and their liberties will be always fecure.

I think we are now arrived to a new æra in the affairs of men, when the true principles of government will be more fully unfolded than heretofore, and a new world, as it were, grow up in America. In contemplating reprefentation, the next thing is the fecurity of elections. Before I proceed to this, I beg leave to obferve, that the pay of the reprefentatives of the people is effentially connected with their interefts.

Congrefs may put the pay of the members unreafonably high, or fo low as that none but the rich and opulent can attend ; there are very ftrong reafons for fuppofing the latter, probably, will be the cafe, and a part of the fame policy, which uniformly and conftantly exerts itfelf to transfer power from the many to the few. Should the pay be well fixed, and made alterable by congrefs, with the confent of a majority of the ftate legiflatures, perhaps, all the evils to be feared on this head might, in the beft practicable manner, be guarded againft, and proper fecurity introduced. It is faid the ftate legiflatures fix their own pay—the anfwer is, that congrefs is not, nor can it ever be well formed on thofe equal principles the ftate legiflatures are. I fhall not dwell on this point, but conclude this letter with one general obfervation, that the check I contend for in the fyftem propofed, do not
:-

in the leaft, any of them tend to leffen the energy of
it ; but giving grounds for the confidence of the people, greatly to increafe its real energy, by infuring their
conftant and hearty fupport.

The FEDERAL FARMER.

LETTER XI.

JANUARY 10, 1788.

Dear Sir,

I SHALL now add a few obfervations refpecting
the organization of the fenate, the manner of appointing it, and its powers.

The fenate is an affembly of 26 members, two from
each ftate, though the fenators are apportioned on the federal plan, they will vote individually ; they reprefent the
ftates, as bodies politic, fovereign to certain purpofes ;
the ftates being fovereign and independent, are all confidered equal, each with the other in the fenate. In
this we are governed folely by the ideal equalities of
fovereignties ; the federal and ftate governments forming one whole, and the ftate governments an effential
part, which ought always to be kept diftinctly in view,
and preferved : I feel more difpofed, on reflection, to
acquiefce in making them the bafis of the fenate, and
thereby to make it the intereft and duty of the fenators
to preferve diftinct, and to perpetuate the refpective
fovereignties they fhall reprefent.

As to the appointments of fenators, I have already
obferved, that they muft be appointed by the legiflatures, by concurrent acts, and each branch have an
equal fhare of power, as I do not fee any probability of
amendments, if advifable, in thefe points, I fhall not
dwell upon them.

The fenate, as a legiflative branch, is not large, but
as an executive branch quite too numerous. It is not
to be prefumed that we can form a genuine fenatorial

I   branch

branch in the United States, a real reprefentation of the ariftocracy and balance in the legiflature, any more than we can form a genuine reprefentation of the people. Could we feparate the ariftocratical and democratical intereſts ; compoſe the ſenate of the former, and the houſe of affembly of the latter, they are too unequal in the United States to produce a balance. Form them on pure principles, and leave each to be fupported by its real weight and connections, the fenate would be feeble, and the houfe powerful :—I fay, on pure principles ; becauſe I make a diftinction between a fenate that derives its weight and influence from a pure fource, its numbers and wifdom, its extenſive property, its extenſive and permanent connections; and a fenate compoſed of a few men, poffeffing fmall property, fmall and unftable connections, that derives its weight and influence from a corrupt or pernicious fource ; that is, merely from the power given it by the conftitution and laws, to difpofe of the public offices, and the annexed emoluments, and by thofe means to intereſt officers, and the hungry expectants of offices, in fupport of its meafures. I wifh the propoſed fenate may not partake too much of the latter defcription.

To produce a balance and checks, the conftitution propoſes two branches in the legiflature ; but they are fo formed, that the members of both muft generally be the fame kind of men—men having fimilar interefts and and views, feelings and connections—men of the fame grade in fociety, and who affociate on all occafions (probably, if there be any difference, the fenators will be the moft democratic.) Senators and reprefentatives thus circumftanced, as men, though convened in two rooms, to make laws, muft be governed generally by the fame motives and views, and therefore purfue the fame fyftem of politics ; the partitions between the two branches will be merely thofe of the building in which they fit : there will not be found in them any of thofe genuine balances and checks, among the real different interefts, and efforts of the feveral claffes of men in the community we aim at ; nor can any fuch balances and checks be formed in the prefent condition of the United

States

States in any confiderable degree of perfection: but to give them the greateft degree of perfection practicable, we ought to make the fenate refpectable as to numbers, the qualifications of the electors and of the elected; to increafe the numbers of the reprefentatives, and fo to model the elections of them, as always to draw a majority of them fubftantially from the body of the people. Though I conclude the fenators and reprefentatives will not form in the legiflature thofe balances and checks which correfpond with the actual ftate of the people; yet I approve of two branches, becaufe we may notwith-ftanding derive feveral advantages from them. The fenate, from the mode of its appointment, will probably be influenced to fupport the ftate governments, and, from its periods of fervice will produce ftability in legiflation, while frequent elections may take place in the other branch. There is generally a degree of competition between two affemblies even compofed of the fame kind of men; and by this, and by means of every law's paffing a revifion in the fecond branch, caution, coolnefs, and deliberation are produced in the bufinefs of making laws. By means of a democratic branch we may particularly fecure perfonal liberty; and by means of a fenatorial branch we may particularly protect property. By the divifion, the houfe becomes the proper body to impeach all officers for mifconduct in office, and the fenate the proper court to try them; and in a country where limited powers muft be lodged in the firft magiftrate, the fenate, perhaps, may be the moft proper body to be found to have a negative upon him in making treaties, and in managing foreign affairs.

Though I agree the federal fenate, in the form propofed, may be ufeful to many purpofes, and that it is not very neceffary to alter the organization, modes of appointment, and powers of it in feveral refpects; yet, without alterations in others, I fincerely believe it will, in a very few years, become the fource of the greateft evils. Some of thefe alterations, I conceive, to be abfolutely neceffary, and fome of them at leaft advifable.

1. By the confederation the members of congrefs are chofen annually. By art. 1. fect. 2. of the conftitu-

tion, the senators shall be chosen for six years. As the period of service must be, in a considerable degree, matter of opinion on this head, I shall only make a few observations, to explain why I think it more advisable to limit it to three or four years.

The people of this country have not been accustomed to so long appointments in their state governments, they have generally adopted annual elections. The members of the present congress are chosen yearly, who, from the nature and multipicity of their business, ought to be chosen for longer periods then the federal senators — Men six years in office absolutely contract callous habits, and cease, in too great a degree, to feel their dependance, and for the condition of their constituents. Senators continued in offices three or four years, will be in them longer than any popular erroneous opinions will probably continue to actuate their electors—men appointed for three or four years, will generally be long enough in office to give stability, and amply to acquire political information. By a change of legislators, as often as circumstances will permit, political knowledge is diffused more extensively among the people, and the attention of the electors and elected more constantly kept alive ; circumstances of infinite importance in a free country. Other reasons might be added, but my subject is too extensive to admit of my dwelling upon less material points.

2. When the confederation was formed, it was considered essentially necessary that the members of congress should at any time be recalled by their respective states, when the states should see fit, and others be sent in their room. I do not think it less necessary that this principle should be extended to the members of congress under the new constitution, and especially to the senators. 1 have had occasion several times to observe, that let us form a federal constitution as extensively, and on the best principles in our power, we must, after all, trust a vast deal to a few men, who, far removed from their constituents, will administer the federal government ; there is but little danger these men will feel too great a degree of dependance : the necessary and important

portant object to be attended to, is to make them feel
dependant enough. Men elected for several years, several hundred miles diftant from their ftates, poffeffed
of very extenfive powers, and the means of paying themfelves, will not, probably, be oppreffed with a fenfe of
dependance and refponfibility.

The fenators will reprefent fovereignties, which generally have, and always ought to retain, the power of
recalling their agents ; the principle of refponfibility is
ftrongly felt in men who are liable to be recalled and
cenfured for their mifconduct ; and, if we may judge
from experience, the latter will not abufe the power of
recalling their members ; to poffefs it, will, at leaft be
a valuable check. It is in the nature of all delegated
power, that the conftituents fhould retain the right to
judge concerning the conduct of their reprefentatives ;
they muft exercife the power, and their decifion itfelf,
their approving or difapproving that conduct implies a
right, a power to continue in office, or to remove from
it. But whenever the fubftitute acts under a conftitution, then it becomes neceffary that the power of recalling him be expreffed. The reafons for lodging a power
to recall are ftronger, as they refpect the fenate, than
as they refpect the reprefentatives ; the latter will be
more frequently elected, and changed of courfe, and
being chofen by the people at large, it would be more
difficult for the people than for the legiflatures to take
the neceffary meafures for recalling : but even the people, if the powers will be more beneficial to them than
injurious, ought to poffefs it. The people are not apt
to wrong a man who is fteady and true to their interefts ;
they may for a while be mifled by party reprefentations,
and leave a good man out of office unheard ; but every
recall fuppofes a deliberate decifion, and a fair hearing ;
and no man who believes his conduct proper, and the
refult of honeft views, will be the lefs ufeful in his public character, on account of the examination his actions
may be liable to ; and a man confcious of the contrary
conduct, ought clearly to be reftrained by the apprehen-
fions of a trial. I repeat it, it is interefted combinations and factions we are particularly to guard againft

is the federal government, and all the rational means
that can be put into the hands of the people to prevent
them, ought to be provided and furnished for them.
Where there is a power to recall, trusty centinels among
the people, or in the state legislatures, will have a fair
opportunity to become useful. If the members in congress from the states join in such combinations, or favour
them, or pursue a pernicious line of conduct, the most
attentive among the people, or in the state legislatures,
may formally charge them before their constituents:
the very apprehensions of such constitutional charges
may prevent many of the evils mentioned, and the recalling the members of a single state, a single senator,
or representative, may often prevent many more; nor
do I, at present, discover any danger in such proceedings, as every man who shall move for a recall will put
his reputation at stake, to shew he has reasonable grounds
for his motion; and it is not probable such motions
will be made unless there be good apparent grounds for
succeeding; nor can the charge or motion be any thing
more than the attack of an individual or individuals,
unless a majority of the constituents shall see cause to
go into the enquiry. Further, the circumstance of such
a power being lodged in the constituents, will tend
continually to keep up their watchfulness, as well as the
attention and dependance of the federal senators and representatives.

3. By the confederation it is provided, that no delegate shall serve more than three years in any term of
six years, and thus, by the forms of the government,
a rotation of members is produced: a like principle has
been adopted in some of the state governments, and
also in some antient and modern republics. Whether
this exclusion of a man for a given period, after he shall
have served a given time, ought to be ingrafed into a
constitution or not, is a question, the proper decision
materially depends upon the leading features of the government: some governments are so formed as to produce a sufficient fluctuation and change of members of
course, in the ordinary course of elections, proper
numbers of new members are, from time to time,
brought

brought into the legiflature, and a proportionate number of old ones go out, mix, and become diffufed
among the people. This is the cafe with all numerous
reprefentative legiflatures, the members of which are
frequently elected, and conftantly within the view of
their conftituents. This is the cafe with our ftate governments, and in them a conftitutional rotation is unimportant. But in a government confifting of but a
few members, elected for long periods, and far removed
from the obfervation of the people, but few changes in
the ordinary courfe of elections take place among the
members; they become in fome meafure a fixed body,
and often inattentive to the public good, callous, felfifh, and the fountain of corruption. To prevent thefe
evils, and to force a principle of pure animation into
the federal government, which will be formed much in
this laft manner mentioned, and to produce attention,
activity, and a diffufion of knowledge in the community, we ought to eftablifh among others the principle
of rotation. Even good men in office, in time, imperceptibly lofe fight of the people, and gradually fall
into meafures prejudicial to them. It is only a rotation
among the members of the federal legiflature I fhall
contend for : judges and officers at the heads of the
judicial and executive departments, are in a very different fituation, their offices and duties require the information and ftudies of many years for performing
them in a manner advantageous to the people. Thefe
judges and officers muft apply their whole time to the
detail bufinefs of their offices, and depend on them for
their fupport then they always act under mafters or
fuperiors, and may be removed from office for mifconduct ; they purfue a certain round of executive bufinefs :
their offices muft be in all focieties confined to a few
men, becaufe but few can become qualified to fill them :
and were they by annual appointments, open to the
people at large, they are offices of fuch a nature as to
be of no fervice to them ; they muft leave thefe offices in the poffeffion of the few individuals qualified to
fill them, or have them badly filled. In the judicial
and executive department: alfo, the body of the people

ple poſſeſs a large ſhare of power and influence, as jurors
and ſubordinate officers, among whom there are many and
frequent rotations. But in every free country the legiſlatures are all on a level, and legiſlation becomes partial
whenever, in practice, it reſts for any conſiderable time in
a few hands. It is the true republican principle to dif-
fuſe the power of making the laws among the people,
and ſo to modify the forms of the government as to draw
in turn the well informed of every claſs into the legiſlature.

To determine the propriety or impropriety of this
rotation, we muſt take the inconveniencies as well as
the advantages attending it into view : on the one hand,
by this rotation, we may ſometimes exclude good men
from being elected. On the other hand, we guard
againſt thoſe pernicious connections, which uſually
grow up among men left to continue long periods in
office, we increaſe the number of thoſe who make the
laws and return to their conſtituents ; and thereby
ſpread information, and preſerve a ſpirit of activity
and inveſtigation among the people : hence a balance of
intereſts and exertions are preſerved, and the ruinous
meaſures of factions rendered more impracticable. I
would not urge the principle of rotation, if I believed
the conſequence would be an uninformed federal legiſlature ; but I have no apprehenſion of this in this enlightened country. The members of congreſs, at any
one time, muſt be but very few, compared with the
reſpectable well informed men in the United States ;
and I have no idea there will be any want of ſuch men
for members of congreſs, though by a principle of rotation the conſtitution ſhould exclude from being elected
for two years thoſe federal legiſlators, who may have
ſerved the four years immediately preceding, or any
four years in the ſix preeeding years. If we may
judge from experience and fair calculations, this principle will never operate to exclude at any one period a
fifteenth part, even of thoſe men who have been members of congreſs. Though no man can ſit in congreſs,
by the confederation, more than three years in any term
of ſix years, yet not more than three, four, or five men
in

in any one ftate, have been made ineligible at any one
period ; and if a good man happen to be excluded by
this rotation, it is only for a fhort time. All things
confidered, the inconveniencies of the principle muft
be very inconfiderable compared with the many advantages of it. It will generally be expedient for a man
who has ferved four years in congrefs to return home,
mix with the people, and refide fome time with them :
this will tend to reinftate him in the interefts, feelings, and
views fimilar to theirs, and thereby confirm in him the
effential qualifications of a legiflator. Even in point of
information, it may be obferved, the ufeful information
of legiflators is not acquired merely in ftudies in offices,
and in meeting to make laws from day to day ; they
muft learn the actual fituation of the people, by being
among them, and when they have made laws, return
home, and obferve how they operate. Thus occafionally
to be among the people, is not only neceffary to prevent
or banifh the callous habits and felf interefted views of
office in legiflators, but to afford them neceffary information, and to render them ufeful : another valuable
end is anfwered by it, fympathy, and the means of
communication between them and their conftituents, is
fubftantially promoted ; fo that on every principle legiflators, at certain periods, ought to live among their conftituents.

Some men of fcience are undoubtedly neceffary in every
legiflature ; but the knowledge, generally, neceffary for
men who make laws, is a knowledge of the common
concerns, and particular circumftances of the people. In
a republican government feats in the legiflature are highly honorable ; I believe but few do, and furely none
ought to confider them as places of profit and permanent
fupport. Were the people alwaye properly attentive,
they would, at proper periods, call their law makers
home, by fending others in their room : but this is not
often the cafe, and therefore, in making conftitutions,
when the people are attentive, they ought cautioufly to
provide for thofe benefits, thofe advantageous changes
in the adminiftration of their affairs, which they are
often apt to be inattentive to in practice. On the

K   whole,

whole, to guard againſt the evils, and to ſecure the advantages I have mentioned, with the greateſt degree of certainty, we ought clearly, in my opinion, to increaſe the federal repreſentation, to ſecure elections on proper principles, to eſtabliſh a right to recall members, and a rotation among them.

4. By the art. 2. ſect. 2. treaties muſt be made with the advice and conſent of the ſenate, and two-thirds of thoſe preſent muſt concur: alſo, with conſent of the ſenate, almoſt all federal officers, civil and military, muſt be appointed. As to treaties I have my doubts; but as to the appointments of officers, 1 think we may clearly ſhew the ſenate to be a very improper body indeed to have any thing to do with them. I am not perfectly ſatisfied, that the ſenate, a branch of the legiſlature, and court for trying impeachments, ought to have a controuling power in making all treaties; yet, I confeſs, I do not diſcern how a reſtraint upon the preſident in this important buſineſs, can be better or more ſafely lodged: a power to make and conclude all treaties is too important to be veſted in him alone, or in him and an executive council, only ſufficiently numerous for other purpoſe, and the houſe of repreſentatives is too numerous to be concerned in treaties of peace and of alliance. This power is now lodged in congreſs, to be exerciſed by the conſent of nine ſtates. The federal ſenate, like the delegations in the preſent congreſs, will repreſent the ſtates, and the conſent of two-thirds of that ſenate will bear ſome ſimilitude to the conſent of nine ſtates. It is probable the United States will not make more than one treaty, on an average, in two or three years, and this power may always be exerciſed with great deliberation: perhaps the ſenate is ſufficiently numerous to be truſted with this power, ſufficiently ſmall to proceed with ſecrecy, and ſufficiently permanent to exerciſe this power with proper conſiſtency and due deliberation. To lodge this power in a leſs reſpectable and leſs numerous body might not be ſafe; we muſt place great confidence in the hands that hold it, and we deceive ourſelves if we give it under an idea, that we can impeach, to any valuable purpoſe, the man or men who may abuſe it.   On

On a fair conftruction of the conftitution, I think the legiflature has a proper controul over the prefident and fenate in fettling commercial treaties. By art. 1. fect. 2. the legiflature will have power to regulate commerce with foreign nations, &c. By art. 2. fect. 2. the prefident, with the advice and confent of two-thirds of the fenate, may make treaties. Thefe claufes muft be confidered together, and we ought never to make one part of the fame inftrument contradict another, if it can be avoided by any reafonable conftruction. By the firft recited claufe, the legiflature has the power, that is, as I underftand it, the fole power to regulate commerce with foreign nations, or to make all the rules and regulations refpecting trade and commerce between our citizens and foreigners : by the fecond recited claufe, the prefident and fenate have power generally to make treaties.— There are feveral kinds of treaties—as treaties of commerce, of peace, of alliance, &c. I think the words to " make treaties," may be confiftently conftrued, and yet fo as it fhall be left to the legiflature to confirm commercial treaties ; they are in their nature and operation very diftinct from treaties of peace and of alliance ; the latter generally require fecrecy, it is but very feldom they interfere with the laws and internal police of the country ; to make them is propeily the exercife of executive powers, and the conftitution authorifes the prefident and fenate to make treaties, and gives the legiflature no power, directly or indirectly, refpecting thefe treaties of peace and alliance. As to treaties of commerce, they do not generally require fecrecy, they almoft always involve in them legiflative powers, interfere with the laws and internal police of the country, and operate immediately on perfons and property, efpecially in the commercial towns : (they have in Great-Britain ufually been confirmed by parliament ;) they confift of rules and regulations refpecting commerce ; and to regulate commerce, or to make regulations refpecting commerce, the federal legiflature, by the conftitution, has the power. I do not fee that any commercial regulations can be made in treaties, that will not infringe upon this power in the legiflature : therefore, I infer, that
the

the true conftruction is, that the prefident and fenate
fhall make treaties ; but all commercial treaties fhall be
fubject to be confirmed by the legiflature. This conftruction will render the claufes confiftent, and make
the powers of the prefident and fenate, refpecting treaties, much lefs exceptionable.

The FEDERAL FARMER.

L E T T E R   XII.

JANUARY 12, 1788.

DEAR SIR,

ON carefully examining the parts of the propofed
fyftem, refpecting the elections of fenators, and
efpecially of the reprefentatives, they appear to me to be
both ambiguous and very defective. I fhall endeavour to
purfue a courfe of reafoning, which fhall fairly lead to
eftablifhing the impartiality and fecurity of elections,
and then to point out an amendment in this refpect.

It is well obferved by Montefquieu, that in republican governments, the forms of elections are fundamental ; and that it is an effential part of the focial compact, to afcertain by whom, to whom, when, and in
what manner fuffrages are to be given.

Wherever we find the regulation of elections have not
been carefully fixed by the conftitution, or the principles of them, we conftantly fee the legiflatures new modifying its own form, and changing the fpirit of the
government to anfwer partial purpofes.

By the propofed plan it is fixed, that the qualifications of the electors of the federal reprefentatives fhall
be the fame as thofe of the electors of ftate reprenfen-
tatives ; though thefe vary fome in the feveral ftates
the electors are fixed and defignated.

The qualifications of the reprefentatives are alfo fixed
and defignated, and no perfon under 25 years of age,
not an inhabitant of the ftate, and not having been
feven years a citizen of the United States, can be elected ;
the

the clear inference is, that all persons 25 years of age,
and upwards, inhabitants of the state, and having been,
at any period or periods, seven years citizens of the
United States, may be elected representatives. They
have a right to be elected by the constitution, and the
electors have a right to chuse them. This is fixing the
federal representation, as to the elected, on a very broad
basis: it can be no objection to the elected, that they
are Christians, Pagans, Mahometans, or Jews; that
they are of any colour, rich or poor, convict or not:
Hence many men may be elected, who cannot be electors. Gentlemen who have commented so largely upon
the wisdom of the constitution, for excluding from
being elected young men under a certain age, would
have done well to have recollected, that it positively
makes pagans, convicts, &c. eligible. The people
make the constitution; they exclude a few persons, by
certain descriptions, from being elected, and all not
thus excluded are clearly admitted. Now a man 25
years old, an inhabitant of the state, and having been a
citizen of the states seven years, though afterwards
convicted, may be elected, because not within any of
the excluding clauses; the same of a beggar, an absen-
tee, &c.

The right of the electors, and eligibility of the elected being fixed by the people, they cannot be narrowed
by the state legislatures, or congress: it is established,
that a man being (among other qualifications) an inhabitant of the state, shall be eligible. Now it would be
narrowing the right of the people to confine them in
their choice to a man, an inhabitant of a particular
county or district in the state. Hence it follows, that
neither the state legislatures or congress can establish
district elections; that is, divide the state into districts,
and confine the electors of each district to the choice of
a man resident in it. If the electors could be thus limited in one respect, they might in another be confined
to chuse a man of a particular religion, of certain property, &c. and thereby half of the persons made eligible
by the constitution be excluded. All laws, therefore,
for regulating elections must be made on the broad basis
of the constitution.

L

Next

Next, we may obferve, that reprefentatives are to be
chofen by the people of the ftate. What is a choice
by the people of the ftate ? If each given diftrict in it
choofe one, will that be a choice within the meaning
of the conftitution ? Muft the choice be by plurality
of votes, or a majority ? In connection with thefe queftions, we muft take the 4th fect. art. 1. where it is
faid the ftate legiflatures fhall prefcribe the times, places,
and manner of holding elections; but congrefs may
make or alter fuch regulations. By this claufe, I fuppofe, the electors of different towns and diftricts in the
ftate may be affembled in different places, to give their
votes; but when fo affembled, by another claufe they
cannot, by congrefs or the ftate legiflatures, be reftrained from giving their votes for any man an inhabitant
of the ftate, and qualified as to age, and having been
a citizen tne time required. But I fee nothing in the
conftitution by which to decide, whether the choice
fhall be by a plurality or a majority of votes : this, in
my mind, is by far the moft important queftion in the
bufinefs of elections. When we fay a reprefentative
fhall be chofen by the people, it feems to imply that
he fhall be chofen by a majority of them ; but ftates
which ufe the fame phrafeology in this refpect, practice
both ways. I believe a majority of the ftates, chufe by
pluralities, and, I think it probable, that the federal
houfe of reprefentatives will decide that a choice of its
members by pluralities is conftitutional. A man who
has the moft votes is chofen in Great-Britain. It is
this, among other things, that gives every man fair
play in the game of influence and corruption. I believe
that not much ftrefs was laid upon the objection that
congrefs may affemble the electors at fome out of the
way place. However, the advocates feem to think
they obtain a victory of no fmall glory and importance, when they can fhew, with fome degree of colour,
that the evils is rather a poffibility than a probability.

When I obferved that the elections were not fecured on
proper principles, I had an idea of far more probable and
extenfive evils, fecret mifchiefs, and not fo glaring
tranfgreffions,

tranfgreffions, the exclufions of proper diftrict elections, and of the choice by a majority.

It is eafy to perceive that there is an effential difference between elections by pluralities and by majorities, between choofing a man in a fmall or limited diftrict, and choofing a number of men promifcuoufly by the people of a large ftate ; and while we are almoft fecure of judicious unbiaffed elections by majorities in fuch diftricts, we have no fecurity againft deceptions, influence and corruption in ftates or large diftricts in electing by pluralities. When a choice is made by a plurality of votes, it is often made by a very fmall part of the electors, who attend and give their votes, when by a majority, never by fo few as one half of them. The partialities and improprieties attending the former mode may be illuftrated by a cafe that lately happened in one of the middle ftates.—Several reprefentatives were to be chofen by a large number of inhabitants compactly fettled, among whom there were four or five thoufand voters. Previous to the time of election a number of lifts of candidates were publifhed, to divide and diftract the voters in general—about half a dozen men of fome influence, who had a favourite lift to carry, met feveral times, fixed their lift, and agreed to hand it about among all who could probably be induced to adopt it, and to circulate the other lifts among their opponents, to divide them. The poll was opened, and feveral hundred electors, fufpecting nothing, attended and put in their votes; the lift of the half dozen was carried, and men were found to be chofen, fome of whom were very difagreeable to a large majority of the electors : though feveral hundred electors voted, men on that lift were chofen who had only 45, 43, 44, &c. votes each ; they had a plurality, that is, more than any other perfons : the votes generally were fcattered, and thofe who made even a feeble combination fucceeded in placing higheft upon the lift feveral very unthought of and very unpopular men. This evil never could have happened in a town where all the voters meet in one place, and confider no man as elected unlefs he have a majority, or more than half of all the votes; clear it

is,

is, that the men on whom thus but a small part of the votes are bestowed, cannot possess the confidence of the people, or have any considerable degree of influence over them.

But as partial, as liable to secret influence, and corruption as the choice by pluralities may be, I think, we cannot avoid it, without essentially increasing the federal representation, and adopting the principles of district elections. There is but one case in which the choice by the majority is practicable, and that is, where districts are formed of such moderate extent that the electors in each can conveniently meet in one place, and at one time, and proceed to the choice of a representative ; when, if no man have a majority, or more than half of all the votes the first time, the voters may examine the characters of those brought forward, accommodate, and proceed to repeat their votes till some one shall have that majority. This, I believe, cannot be a case under the constitution proposed in its present form. To explain my ideas, take Massachusetts, for instance, she is entitled to eight representatives, she has 370,000 inhabitants, about 46,000 to one representative ; if the elections be so held that the electors throughout the state meet in their several towns or places, and each elector puts in his vote for eight representatives, the votes of the electors will ninety-nine times in a hundred, be so scattered that on collecting the votes from the several towns or places, no men will be found, each of whom have a majority of the votes, and therefore the election will not be made. On the other hand, there may be such a combination of votes, that in thus attempting to chuse eight representatives, the electors may chuse even fifteen. Suppose 10,000 voters to attend and give their votes, each voter will give eight votes, one for each of eight representatives; in the whole 80,000 votes will be given—eight men, each having 5001 votes, in the whole 40,008 will have each a majority, and be chosen—39 092 votes will be bestowed on other men, and if they all be bestowed on seven men, they may have each a considerable majority, and also be chosen. This indeed

is

is a very rare combination: but the beftowing all the
votes pretty equally upon nine, ten, or eleven men, and
chufing them all, is an event too probable not to be
guarded againft.

If Maffachufetts be divided into eight diftricts, each
having about 46,000 inhabitants, and each diftrict directed to chufe one reprefentative, it will be found
totally impracticable for the electors of it to meet in
one place ; and, when they meet in feveral towns and
places in the diftrict, they will vote for different men,
and nineteen times in twenty, fo fcatter their votes, that
no one man will have a majority of the whole and be
chofen : we muft, therefore, take the man who has the
moft votes, whether he has three quarters, one quarter,
or one tenth part of the whole ; the inconveniencies
of fcattering votes will be increafed, as men not of the
diftrict, as well as thofe that are in it, may be voted
for.

I might add many other obfervations to evince the
fuperiority and folid advantages of proper diftrict elections, and a choice by a majority, and to prove, that
many evils attend the contrary practice : thefe evils we
muft encounter as the conftitution now ftands.

I fee no way to fix elections on a proper footing, and
to render tolerably equal and fecure the federal reprefentation, but by increafing the reprefentation, fo as to
have one reprefentative for each diftrict, in which the
electors may conveniently meet in one place, and at one
time, and chufe by a majority. Perhaps this might be
effected pretty generally, by fixing one reprefentative
for each twelve thoufand inhabitants ; dividing, or fixing
the principles for dividing the ftates into proper diftricts;
and directing the electors of each diftrict to the choice,
by a majority, of fome men having a permanent intereft
and refidence in it. I fpeak of a reprefentation tolerably equal, &c. becaufe I am ftill of opinion, that it is
impracticable in this extenfive country to have a federal
reprefentation fufficiently democratic, or fubftantially
drawn from the body of the people : the principles
juft mentioned may be the beft practical ones we can
expect to eftablifh. By thus increafing the reprefentation

tion, we not only make it more democratical and fecure, ftrengthen the confidence of the people in it, and thereby render it more nervous and energetic ; but it will alfo enable the people effentially to change, for the better, the principles and forms of elections. To provide for the people's wandering throughout the ftate for a repre-fentative, may fometimes enable them to elect a more brilliant or an abler man, than by confining them to diftricts, but generally this latitude will be ufed to per-nicious purpofes, efpecially connected with the choice by plurality ; when a man in the remote part of the ftate, perhaps, obnoxious at home, but ambitious and intriguing, may be chofen to reprefent the people in another part of the ftate far diftant, and by a fmall part of them, or by a faction, or by a combination of fome particular defcription of men among them. This has been long the cafe in Great-Britain, it is the cafe in feveral of the ftates, nor do I think that fuch pernicious practices will be merely poffible in our federal concerns, but highly probable. By eftablifhing diftrict elections, we exclude none of the beft men from being elected ; and we fix what, in my mind, is of far more importance than brilliant talents, I mean a famenefs, as to refidence and interefts, between the reprefentative and his confti-tuents ; and by the election by a majority, he is fure to be the man, the choice of more than half of them.

Though it is impoffible to put elections on a proper footing as the conftitution ftands, yet I think regula-tions refpecting them may be introduced of confiderable fervice : it is not only, therefore, important to enquire how they may be made, but alfo what body has the con-trouling power over them. An intelligent, free and unbiaffed choice of reprefentatives by the people is of the laft importance : we muft then carefully guard againft all combinations, fecret arts, and influence to the contrary. Various expedients have been adopted in different countries and ftates to effect genuine elections; as the conftitution now ftands, I confefs, I do not dif-cover any better than thofe adopted in Connecticut, in the choice of counfellers, before mentioned.

The

The federal reprefentatives are to be chofen every fecond year (an odd mode of expreffion). In all the ftates, except South-Carolina, the people, the fame electors, meet twice in that time to elect ftate reprefentatives. For inftance, let the electors in Maffachufetts, when they meet to chufe ftate reprefentatives, put in their votes for eight federal reprefentatives, the number that ftate may chufe, (merely for diftinction fake, we may call thefe the votes of nomination), and return a lift of the men voted for, in the feveral towns and places, to the legiflature, or fome proper body; let this lift be immediately examined and publifhed, and fome proper number, fay 15 or 20, who fhall have the moft votes upon the lift, be fent out to the people; and when the electors fhall meet the next year to chufe ftate reprefentatives, let them put in their votes for the eight federal reprefentatives, confining their votes to the proper number fo fent out; and let the eight higheft of thofe thus voted for in the two votes (which we may call, by way of diftinction, votes of election), be the federal reprefentatives: thus a choice may be made by the people, once in two years, without much trouble and expence, and, I believe, with fome degree of fecurity. As foon as the votes of nomination fhall be collected and made known, the people will know who are voted for, and who are candidates for their votes the fucceeding year; the electors will have near a year to enquire into their characters and politics, and alfo into any undue means, if any were taken, to bring any of them forward; and fuch as they find to be the beft men, and agreeable to the people, they may vote for in giving the votes of election. By thefe means the men chofen will ultimately always have a majority, or near a majority, of the votes of the electors, who fhall attend and give their votes. The mode itfelf will lead to the difcovery of truth and of political characters, and to prevent private combinations, by rendering them in a great meafure of no effect. As the choice is to be made by the people, all combinations and checks muft be confined to their votes. No fupplying the want of a majority by the legiflatures, as in Maffachufetts in the choice of
fenators,

senators, &c. can be admitted : the people generally judge right when informed, and, in giving their votes the second time, they may always correct their former errors.

I think we are all sufficiently acquainted with the progress of elections to see, that the regulations, as to times, places, and the manner merely of holding elections, may, under the constitution, easily be made useful or injurious. It is important then to enquire, who has the power to make regulations, and who ought to have it. By the constitution, the state legislatures shall prescribe the times, places, and manner of holding elections, but congress may make or alter such regulations. Power in congress merely to alter those regulations, made by the states, could answer no valuable purposes ; the states might make, and congress alter them *ad infinitum :* and when the state should cease to make, or should annihilate its regulations, congress would have nothing to alter. But the states shall make regulations, and congress may make such regulations as the clause stands : the true construction is, that when congress shall see fit to regulate the times, places, and manner of holding elections, congress may do it, and state regulations, on this head, must cease ; for if state regulations could exist, after congress should make a system of regulations, there would, or might, be two incompatible systems of regulations relative to the same subject.

It has been often urged, that congress ought to have power to make these regulations, otherwise the state legislatures, by neglecting to make provision for elections, or by making improper regulations, may destroy the general government. It is very improbable that any state legislature will adopt measures to destroy the representation of its own constituents in congress, especially when the state must, represented in congress or not, pay its proportion of the expence of keeping up the government, and even of the representatives of the other states, and be subject to their laws. Should the state legislatures be disposed to be negligent, or to combine to break up congress, they have a very simple way to do it, as the constitution now stands—
they

they have only to neglect to chufe fenators, or
to appoint the electors of the prefident, and vice-
prefident : there is no remedy provided againft thefe
laft evils : nor is it to be prefumed, that if a fufficient
number of ftate legiflatures to break up congrefs, fhould,
by neglect or otherwife, attempt to do it, that the people, who yearly elect thofe legiflatures, would elect
under the regulations of congrefs. Thefe and many
other reafons muft evince, that it was not merely to
prevent an annihilation of the federal government that
congrefs has power to regulate elections.

It has been urged alfo, that the ftate legiflatures chufe
the federal fenators, one branch, and may injure the
people, who chufe the other, by improper regulations;
that therefore congrefs, in which the people will immediately have one, the reprefentative branch, ought to
have power to interfere in behalf of the people, and
rectify fuch improper regulations. The advocates have
faid much about the opponents dwelling upon poffibi-
lities ; but to fuppofe the people will find it neceffary
to appeal to congrefs to reftrain the oppreffions of the
ftate legiflatures, is fuppofing a poffibility indeed. Can
any man in his fenfes fuppofe that the ftate legiflatures,
which are fo numerous as almoft to be the people themfelves, all branches of them depending yearly, for the
moft part, on the elections of the people, will abufe
them in regulating federal elections, and make it proper
to transfer the power to congrefs, a body, one branch
of which is chofen once in fix years by thefe very legiflatures, and the other biennially and not half fo
numerous as even the fenatorial branches in thofe legiflatures ?

Senators are to be chofen by the ftate legiflatures,
where there are two branches the appointment muft be,
I prefume, by a concurrent refolution, in paffing which,
as in paffing all other legiflative acts each branch will
have a negative ; this will give the fenatorial branch juft
as much weight in the appointment as the democratic :
the two branches form a legiflature only when acting
feparately, and therefore, whenever the members of the
two branches meet, mix and vote individually in one

M

room, for making an election, it is exprefsly fo directed by the conftitutions. If the conftitution, by fixing
the choice to be made by the legiflatures, has given
each branch an equal vote, as I think it has, it cannot
be altered by any regulations.

On the whole, I think, all general principles refpecting electors ought to be carefully eftablifhed by the
conftitution, as the qualifications of the electors and of
elected : the number of the reprefentatives, and the inhabitants of each given diftrict, called on to chufe a
man from among themfelves by a majority of votes ;
leaving it to the legiflature only fo to regulate, from
time to time, the extent of the diftricts fo as to keep the
reprefentatives proportionate to the number of inhabitants in the feveral parts of the country ; and fo far as
regulations as to elections cannot be fixed by the conftitution, they ought to be left to the ftate legiflatures,
they coming far neareft to the people themfelves ; at
moft, congrefs ought to have power to regulate elections
only where a ftate fhall neglect to make them.

THE FEDERAL FARMER.

LETTER XIII.

JANUARY 14, 1788.

DEAR SIR,

IN this letter I fhall further examine two claufes in
the propofed conftitution refpecting appointments to
office.—By art. 2. fect. 2. the prefident fhall nominate,
and by and with the advice and confent of the fenate,
fhall appoint ambaffadors, other public minifters and
confuls, judges of the fupreme court, and all other officers of the United States, whofe appointments, &c.
By art. 1, fect. 6. No fenator or reprefentative fhall,
during the term for which he was elected, be appointed
to any civil office under the authority of the United
States, which fhall have been created, or the emoluments whereof fhall have been increafed duri g fuch

Thus

Thus the prefident muft nominate, and the fe^{nate} concur in the appointment of all federal officers, civil and military, and the fenators and reprefentatives are made ineligible only to the few civil offices abovementioned. To preferve the federal government pure and uncorrupt, peculiar precautions relative to appointments to office will be found highly neceffary from the very forms and character of the government itfelf. The honours and emoluments of public offices are the objects in all communities, that ambitious and neceffitous men never lofe fight of. The honeft, the modeft, and the induftrious part of the community content themfelves, generally, with their private concerns; they do not folicit thofe offices which are the perpetual fource of cabals, intrigues, and contefts among men of the former defcription, men embarraffed, intriguing, and deftitute of modefty. Even in the moft happy country and virtuous government, corrupt influence in appointments cannot always be avoided; perhaps we may boaft of our fhare of virtue as a people, and if we are only fufficiently aware of the influence, biaffes, and prejudices, common to the affairs of men, we may go far towards guarding againft the effects of them.

We all agree, that a large ftanding army has a ftrong tendency to deprefs and inflave the people; it is equally true that a large body of felfifh, unfeeling, unprincipled civil officers has a like, or a more pernicious tendency to the fame point. Military, and efpecially civil eftablifhments, are the neceffary appendages of fociety; they are deductions from productive labour, and fubftantial wealth, in proportion to the number of men employed in them; they are oppreffive where unneceffarily extended and fupported by men unfriendly to the people; they are injurious when too fmall, and fupported by men too timid and dependant. It is of the laft importance to decide well upon the neceffary number of offices, to fill them with proper characters, and to eftablifh efficiently the means of punctually punifhing thofe officers who may do wrong.

To difcern the nature and extent of this power of appointments, we need only to confider the vaft number

of

of officers neceffary to execute a national fyftem in this
extenfive country,- the prodigious biaffes the hopes and
expectations of offices have on their conduct, and the
influence public officers have among the people—
thefe neceffary officers, as judges, ftate's attornies,
clerks, fheriffs, &c. in the federal fupreme and inferior
courts, admirals and generals, and fubordinate officers
in the army and navy minifters, confuls, &c. fent to
foreign countries ; officers in the federal city, in the
revenue, poft office departments, &c. &c. muft, probably, amount to feveral thoufands, without taking into view the very inferior ones. There can be no doubt
but that the moft active men in politics, in and out of
congrefs, will be the foremoft candidates for the beft of
thefe offices ; the man or men who fhall have the difpofal of them, beyond difpute, will have by far the
greateft fhare of active influence in the government ;
but appointments muft be made, and who fhall make them ?
what modes of appointments will be attended with the
feweft inconveniencies ? is the queftion. The fenators and reprefentatives are the law makers, create all
offices, and whenever they fee fit, they impeach and
try officers for mifconduct : they ought to be in feffion
but part of the year, and as legiflators, they muft be too
numerous to make appointments, perhaps, a few very
important ones excepted. In contemplating the neeef-
fary officers of the union, there appear to be fix different modes in which, in whole or in part, the appointments may be made, 1. By the legiflature ; 2. by the
prefident and fenate—3. by the prefident and an executive council—4. by the prefident alone - 5. by the heads
of the departments—and 6. by the ftate governments —
Among all thefe, in my opinion, there may be an advantageous diftribution of the power of appointments.
In confidering the legiflators, in relation to the fubject
before us, two interefting queftions particularly arife—
1. Whether they ought to be eligible to any offices
whatever during the period for which they fhall be
elected to ferve, and even for fome time afterwards—
and 2. How far they ought to participate in the power
of appointments. As to the firft, it is true that legiflators

lators in foreign countries, or in our ftate governments; are not generally made ineligible to office : there are good reafons for it ; in many countries the people have gone on without ever examining the principles of government. There have been but few countries in which the legiflators have been a particular fet of men periodically chofen : but the principal reafon is, that which operates in the feveral ftates, viz. the legiflators are fo frequently chofen, and fo numerous, compared with the number of offices for which they can reafonably confider themfelves as candidates, that the chance of any individual member's being chofen, is too fmall to raife his hopes or expectations, or to have any confiderable influence upon his conduct. Among the ftate legiflators, one man in twenty may be appointed in fome committee bufinefs, &c. for a month or two ; but on a fair computation, not one man in a hundred fent to the ftate legiflatures is appointed to any permanent office of profit : directly the reverfe of this will evidently be found true in the federal adminiftration. Throughout the United States, about four federal fenators, and thirty-three reprefentatives, averaging the elections, will be chofen in a year; thefe few men may rationally confider themfelves as the faireft candidates for a very great number of lucrative offices, which muft become vacant in the year, and pretty clearly a majority of the federal legiflators, if not excluded, will be mere expectants for public offices. I need not adduce further arguments to eftablifh a pofition fo clear , I need only call to your recollection my obfervations in a former letter, wherein I endeavoured to fhew the fallacy of the argument, that the members muft return home and mix with the people. It is faid, that men are governed by interefted motives, and will not attend as legiflators, unlefs they can, in common with others, be eligible to offices of honor and profit. This will undoubtedly be the cafe with fome men, but I prefume only with fuch men as never ought to be chofen legiflators in a free country ; an oppofite principle will influence good men ; virtuous patriots, and generous minds, will efteem it a higher honor to be felected as the guardians of a free people ;

N   they

they will be fatisfied with a reafonable compenfation
for their time and fervice ; nor will they wifh to be
within the vortex of influence. The valuable effects of
this principle of making legiflators ineligible to offices
for a given time, has never yet been fufficiently attended to or confidered ; I am affured, that it was eftablifhed by the convention after long debate, and afterwards, on an unfortunate change of a few members,
altered. Could the federal legiflators be excluded in
the manner propofed, I think it would be an important
point gained ; as to themfelves, they would be left to
act much more from motives confiftent with the public
good.

In confidering the principle of rotation I had occafion to diftinguifh the condition of a legiflator from
that of mere official man—We acquire certain habits,
feelings, and opinions, as men and citizens—others,
and very different ones, from a long continuance in office : It is, therefore, a valuable obfervation in many
bills of rights, that rulers ought frequently to return
and mix with the people. A legiflature, in a free
country, muft be numerous ; it is in fome degree a periodical affemblage of the people, frequently formed
—the principal officers in the executive and judicial
departments, muft have more permanency in office   Hence it may be inferred, that the legiflature
will remain longer uncorrupted and virtuous ; longer
congenial to the people, than the officers of thofe departments. If it is not, therefore, in our power to
preferve republican principles, for a feries of ages, in
all the departments of government, we may a long
while preferve them in a well formed legiflature. To this
end we ought to take every precaution to prevent legiflators becoming mere office-men ; chufe them frequently, make them recallable, eftablifh rotation among
them. make them ineligible to offices, and give them
as fmall a fhare as poffible in the difpofal of them.
Add to this, a legiflature, in the nature of things, is
not formed for the detail bufinefs of appointing officers ;
there is alfo generally an impropriety in the fame men's
making offices and filling them, and a ftill greater impropriety

propriety in their impeaching and trying the officers they appoint. For thefe, and other reafons, I con-clude, the legiflature is not a proper body for the ap-pointment of officers in general. But having gone through with the different modes of appointment, I fhall endeavour to fhew what fhare in the diftribution of the power of appointments the legiflature muft, from neceffity, rather than from propriety, take. 2. Officers may be appointed by the prefident and fenate—this mode, for general purpofes, is clearly not defenfible. All the reafoning touching the legiflature will apply to the fenate ; the fenate is a branch of the legiflature, which ought to be kept pure and unbiaffed ; it has a part in trying officers for mifconduct, and in creating offices, it is too numerous for a council of appointment, or to feel any degree of refponfibility : if it has an ad-vantage of the legiflature, in being the leaft numerous, jt has a difadvantage in being more unfafe : add to this, the fenate is to have a fhare in the important branch of power refpecting treaties. Further, this fexennial fe-nate of 26 members, reprefenting 13 fovereign ftates, will not, in practice, be found to be a body to advife, but to order and dictate in fact ; and the prefident will be a mere *primus inter pares.* The confequence will be, that the fenate, with thefe efficient means of influ-ence, will not only dictate, probably, to the prefident, but manage the houfe, as the conftitution now ftands ; and under appearances of a balanced fyftem, in reality, govern alone. There may alfo, by this undue connec-tion, be particular periods when a very popular prefi-dent may have a very improper influence upon the fe-nate and upon the legiflature A council of appoint-ment muft ve y probably fit all, or near all, the year—the fenate will be too important and too expenfive a body for this. By giving the fenate, directly or indi-rectly, an undue influence over the reprefentatives, and the improper means of fettering, embarraffing, or con-trouling the prefident or executive, we give the govern-ment, in the very out fet, a fatal and pernicious tendency to that middle undefirable point—ariftocracy. When we, as a circumftance not well to be avoided, admit the

N 2

fenate

senate to a share of power in making treaties, and in managing foreign concerns, we certainly progress full far enough towards this most undesirable point in government. For with this power, also, I believe, we must join that of appointing ambassadors, other foreign ministers, and consuls, being powers necessarily connected.—In every point of view, in which I can contemplate this subject, it appears extremely clear to me, that the senate ought not generally to be a council of appointment. The legislature, after the people, is the great fountain of power, and ought to be kept as pure and uncorrupt as possible, from the hankerings, biasses, and contagion of offices—then the streams issuing from it, will be less tainted with those evils. It is not merely the number of impeachments, that are to be expected to make public officers honest and attentive in their business. A general opinion must pervade the community, that the house, the body to impeach them for misconduct, is disinterested, and ever watchful for the public good ; and that the judges who shall try impeachments, will not feel a shadow of bias. Under such circumstances, men will not dare transgress, who, not deterred by such accusers and judges, would repeatedly misbehave. We have already suffered many and extensive evils, owing to the defects of the confederation, in not providing against the misconduct of public officers. When we expect the law to be punctually executed, not one man in ten thousand will disobey it : it is the probable chance of escaping punishment that induces men to transgress. It is one important mean to make the government just and honest, rigidly and constantly to hold, before the eyes of those who execute it, punishment, and dismission from office, for misconduct. These are principles no candid man, who has just ideas of the essential features of a free government, will controvert. They are, to be sure, at this period, called visionary, speculative and anti-governmental – but in the true stile of courtiers. selfish politicians, and flatterers of despotism —discerning republican men of both parties see their value. They are said to be of no value, by empty boasting advocates for the constitution, who, by their

weakness

weaknefs and conduct, in fact, injure its caufe much more than moft of its opponents. From their high founding promifes, men are led to expect a defence of it, and to have their doubts removed. When a number of long pieces appear, they, inftead of the defence, &c. they expected, fee nothing but a parade of names— volumes written without ever coming to the point—cafes quoted between which and ours there is not the leaft fimilitude—and partial extracts made from hiftories and governments, merely to ferve a purpofe. Some of them, like the true admirers of royal and fenatorial robes, would fain prove, that nations who have thought like freemen and philofophers about government, and endeavoured to be free, have often been the moft miferable : if a fingle riot, in the courfe of five hundred years happened in a free country, if a falary, or the intereft of a public or private debt was not paid at the moment, they feem to lay more ftrefs upon thefe triffles (for triffles they are in a free and happy country) than upon the oppreffions of defpotic government for ages together. As to the lengthy writer in New-York you mention, I have attentively examined his pieces ; he appears to be a candid good-hearted man, to have a good ftile, and fome plaufible ideas ; but when we carefully examine his pieces, to fee where the ftrength of them lies ; when the mind endeavours to fix on thofe material parts, which ought to be the effence of all voluminous productions, we do not find them : the writer appears conftantly to move on a fmooth furface, the part of his work, like the parts of a cob-houfe, are all equally ftrong and all equally weak, and all like thofe works of the boys, without an object ; his pieces appear to have but little relation to the great queftion, whether the conftitution is fitted to the condition and character of this people or not. But to return—3 Officers may be appointed by the prefident and an executive council — when we have affigned to the legiflature the appointment of a few important officers—to the prefident and fenate the appointment of thofe concerned in managing foreign affairs—to the ftate governments the appointment of militia officers, and authorife the legiflature by

legiflative

legiflative acts, to affign to the prefident alone, to the heads of the departments, and courts of law refpectively, the appointment of many inferior officers; we fhall then want to lodge fome where a refiduum of power, a power to appoint all other neceffary officers, as eftablifhed by law. The fitteft receptacle for this refiduary power is clearly, in my opinion, the firft executive magiftrate, advifed and directed by an executive council of feven or nine members, periodically chofen from fuch proportional diftricts as the union may for the purpofe be divided into. The people may give their votes for twice the number of counfellers wanted, and the federal legiflature take twice the number alfo from the higheft candidates, and from among them chufe the feven or nine, or number wanted. Such a council may be rationally formed for the bufinefs of appointments; whereas the fenate, created for other purpofes, never can be— Such councils forms a feature in fome of the beft executives in the union—they appear to be effential to every firft magiftrate, who may frequently want advice.

To authorife the prefident to appoint his own council would he unfafe: to give the fole appointment of it to the legiflature, would confer an undue and unneceffary influence upon that branch. Such a council for a year would be lefs expenfive than the fenate for four months. The prefident may nominate, and the counfellers always be made refponfible for their advice and opinions, by recording and figning whatever they advife to be done. They and the prefident, to many purpofes, will properly form an independent executive branch; have an influence unmixed with the legiflative, which the executive never can have while connected with a powerful branch of the legiflature. And yet the influence arifing from the power of appointments be lefs dangerous, becaufe in lefs dangerous hands—hands properly adequate to poffefs it. Whereas the fenate, from its character and fituation, will add a dangerous weight to the power itfelf, and be far lefs capable of refponfibility, than the council propofed. There is another advantage the refiduum of power, as to appointments, which the prefident and council need poffefs, is lefs than that the

the prefident and fenate muft have. And as fuch a council would render the feffions of the fenate uaneceffary many months in the year, the expences of the government would not be increafed, if they would not be leffened by the inftitution of fuch a council. I think I need not dwell upon this article, as the fitnefs of this mode of appointment will perhaps amply appear by the evident unfitnefs of the others.

4. Officers may be appointed by the prefident alone. It has been almoft univerfally found, when a man has been authorized to exercife power alone, he has never done it alone ; but, generally, aided his determinations by, and refted on the advice and opinions of others. And it often happens when advice is wanted, the worft men, the moft interefted creatures, the worft advice is at hand, obtrude themfelves, and mifdirect the mind of him who would be informed and advifed. It is very feldom we fee a fingle executive, depend on accidental advice and affiftance ; but each fingle executive has, almoft always, formed to itfelf a regular council, to be affembled and confulted on important occafions : this proves that a felect council, of fome kind, is, by experience, generally found neceffary and ufeful. But in a free country, the exercife of any confiderable branch of power ought to be under fome checks and controuls As to this point, I think the conftitution ftands well, the legiflature may, when it fhall deem it expedient, from time to time, authorife the prefident alone to appoint particular inferior officers, and when neceffary to take back the power. His power, therefore, in this refpect, may always be increafed or decreafed by the legiflature, as experience, the beft inftructor, fhall direct : always keeping him, by the conftitution, within certain bounds.

The FEDERAL FARMER.

LETTER

LETTER XIV.

DEAR SIR,

TO continue the subject of appointments :—Officers, in the fifth place, may be appointed by the heads of departments or courts of law. Art. 2. sect. 2. respecting appointments, goes on---" But congress may by law vest the appointment of such inferior officers as they think proper in the president alone, in the courts of law, or in the heads of departments." The probability is, as the constitution now stands, that the senate, a branch of the legislature, will be tenacious of the power of appointment, and much too sparingly part with a share of it to the courts of law, and heads of departments. Here again the impropriety appears of the senate's having, generally, a share in the appointment of officers. We may fairly presume, that the judges, and principal officers in the departments, will be able well informed men in their respective branches of business; that they will, from experience, be best informed as to proper persons to fill inferior offices in them; that they will feel themselves responsible for the execution of their several branches of business, and for the conduct of the officers they may appoint therein.—From these, and other considerations, I think we may infer, that impartial and judicious appointments of subordinate officers will, generally, be made by the courts of law, and the heads of departments. This power of distributing appointments, as circumstances may require, into several hands, in a well formed disinterested legislature, might be of essential service, not only in promoting beneficial appointments, but, also, in preserving the balance in government : a feeble executive may be strengthened and supported by placing in its hands more numerous appointments ; an executive too influential may be reduced within proper bounds, by placing many of the inferior appointments in the courts of law, and heads of departments ; nor is there much danger that the executive will be wantonly weakened or

strengthened

ſtrengthened by the legiſlature, by thus ſhifting the appointments of inferior officers, ſince all muſt be done
by legiſlative acts, which cannot be paſſed without the
conſent of the executive, or the conſent of two-thirds
of both branches—a good legiſlature will uſe this power
to preſerve the balance and perpetuate the government.
Here again we are brought to our ultimatum :—is the
legiſlature ſo conſtructed as to deſerve our confidence ?

6. Officers may be appointed by the ſtate governments. By art. 1. ſect. 8 the reſpective ſtates are
authoriſed excluſively to appoint the militia-officers.
This not only lodges the appointments in proper places,
but it alſo tends to diſtribute and lodge in different executive hands the powers of appointing to offices, ſo
dangerous when collected into the hands of one or a
few men.

It is a good general rule, that the legiſlative, executive, and judicial powers, ought to be kept diſtinct ;
but this, like other general rules, has its exceptions ;
and without theſe exceptions we cannot form a good
government, and properly balance its parts ; and we
can determine only from reaſon experience and a
critical inſpection of the parts of the government how
far it is proper to intermix thoſe powers. Appointment , I believe, in all mixed governments, have been
aſſigned to different hands—ſome are made by the executive, ſome by the legiſlature, ſome by the judges and
ſome by the people. It has been thought adviſeable by
the wiſeſt nations, that the legiſlature ſhould ſo far exerciſe executive and judicial powers as to appoint ſome
officers, judge of the elections of its members, and impeach and try officers for miſconduct—that the executive ſhould have a partial ſhare in legiſlation—that judges
ſhould appoint ſome ſubordinate officers, and regulate
ſo far as to eſtabliſh rules for their own proceedings.
Where the members of the government, as the houſe,
the ſenate, the executive, and judiciary, are ſtrong and
complete, each in itſelf, the balance is naturally produced, each party may take the powers congenial to
it, and we have leſs need to be anxious about checks,
and the ſubdiviſion of powers.

O

H

If after making the deductions, already alluded to, from the general power to appoint federal officers the residuum shall be thought to be too large and unsafe, and to place an undue influence in the hands of the president and council, a further deduction may be made, with many advantages, and, perhaps, with but a few inconveniencies; and that is, by giving the ap-pointment of a few great officers to the legislature—as of the commissioners of the treasury—of the comptroller, treasurer, master coiner, and some of the principal officers in the money department—of the sheriffs or marshalls of the United States—of states attornies, se-cretary of the home department, and secretary at war, perhaps, of the judges of the supreme court—of major-generals and admirals. The appointments of these offi-cers, who may be at the heads of the great departments of business, in carrying into execution the national sys-tem involve in them a variety of considerations ; they will not often occur, and the power to make them ought to remain in safe hands. Officers of the above description are appointed by the legislatures in some of the states, and in some not. We may, I believe, pre-sume that the federal legislature will possess sufficient knowledge and discernment to make judicious appoint-ments : however, as these appointments by the legisla-ture tend to increase a mixture of power, to lessen the advantages of impeachments and responsibility, I would by no means contend for them any further than it may be necessary for reducing the power of the executive within the bounds of safety. To determine with pro-priety how extensive power the executive ought to pos-sess relative to appointments, we must also examine the forms of it, and its other powers ; and these forms and other powers I shall now proceed briefly to examine.

By art. 2. sect 1. the executive power shall be vest-ed in a president elected for four years, by electors to be appointed from time to time. in such manner as the state legislatures shall direct—the electors to be equal in numbers to the federal senators and representatives : but congress may determine the time of chusing sena-tors, and the day on which they shall give their votes ;

and

and if no prefident be chofen by the electors, by a majority of votes, the ftates, as ftates in congrefs, fhall
elect one of the five higheft on the lift for prefident.
It is to be obferved, that in chufing the prefident, the
principle of electing by a majority of votes is adopted ;
in chufing the vice-prefident, that of electing by a plurality. Viewing the principles and checks eftablifhed
in the election of the prefident, and efpecially confidering the feveral ftates may guard the appointment of
the electors as they fhall judge beft. I confefs there appears to be a judicious combination of principles and
precautions. Were the electors more numerous than
they will be, in cafe the reprefentation be not increafed,
I think, the fyftem would be improved ; not that I
confider the democratic character fo important in the
choice of the electors as in the choice of reprefentatives :
be the electors more or lefs democratic, the prefident
will be one of the very few of the moft elevated characters. But there is danger, that a majority of a fmall
number of electors may be corrupted and influenced,
after appointed electors, and before they give their
votes, efpecially if a confiderable fpace of time elapfe
between the appointment and voting. I have already
confidered the advifory council in the executive branch :
there are two things further in the organization of the
executive, to which I would particularly draw your attention ; the firft, which, is a fingle executive, I confefs, I approve ; the fecond, by which any perfon from
period to period may be re-elected prefident, I think
very exceptionable.

Each ftate in the union has uniformly fhewn its pre-
ference for a fingle executive, and generally directed
the firft executive magiftrate to act in certain cafes by
the advice of an executive council. Reafon, and the
experience of enlightened nations, feem juftly to affign
the bufinefs of making laws to numerous affemblies ;
and the execution of them, principally, to the direction
and care of one man. Independent of practice, a
fingle man feems to be peculiarly well circumftanced to
fuperintend the execution of laws with difcernment and
decifion, with promptitude and uniformity : the people
ufually

uſually point out a firſt man—he is to be ſeen in civilized as well as uncivilized nations—in republics as well as in other governments In every large collection of people there muſt be a viſible point ſerving as a common centre in the government, towards which to draw their eyes and attachments. The conſtitution muſt fix a man, or a congreſs of men, ſuperior in the opinion of the people to the moſt popular men in the different parts of the community, eiſe the people will be apt to divide and follow their reſpective leaders. Aſpiring men, armies and navies, have not often been kept in tolerable order by the decrees of a ſenate or an executive council. The advocates for lodging the executive power in the hands of a number of equals, as an executive council, ſay, that much wiſdom may be collected in ſuch a council, and that it will be ſafe ; but they agree, that it cannot be ſo prompt and reſponſible as a ſingle man—they admit that ſuch a council will generally conſiſt of the ariſtocracy, and not ſtand ſo indifferent between it and the people as a firſt magiſtrate. But the principal objection made to a ſingle man is, that when poſſeſſed of power he will be conſtantly ſtruggling for more, diſturbing the government, and encroaching on the rights of others. It muſt be admitted, that men, from the monarch down to the porter, are conſtantly aiming at power and importance ; and this propenſity muſt be as conſtantly guarded againſt in the forms of the government. Adequate powers muſt be delegated to thoſe who govern, and our ſecurity muſt be in limiting, defining, and guarding the exerciſe of them, ſo that thoſe given ſhall not be abuſed, or made uſe of for openly or ſecretly ſeizing more. Why do we believe this abuſe of power peculiar to a firſt magiſtrate ? Is it becauſe in the wars and conteſts of men, one man has often eſtabliſhed his power over the reſt ? Or are men naturally fond of accumulating powers in the hands of one man ? I do not ſee any ſimilitude between the caſes of thoſe tyrants, who have ſprung up in the midſt of wars and tumults, and the caſes of limited executives in eſtabliſhed governments ; nor ſhall we, on a careful examination, diſcover much likeneſs between the
executives

executives in Sweden, Denmark, Holland, &c. which have, from time to time, increased their powers, and become more absolute, and the executives, whose powers are well ascertained and defined, and which remain, by the constitution, only for a short and limited period in the hands of any one man or family. A single man, or family, can long and effectually direct its exertions to one point. There may be many favourable opportunities in the course of a man's life to seize on additional powers, and many more where powers are hereditary; and there are many circumstances favourable to usurpations, where the powers of the man or family are undefined, and such as often may be unduly extended before the people discover it. If we examine history attentively, we shall find that such exertions, such opportunities, and such circumstances as these have attended all the executives which have usurped upon the rights of the people, and which appear originally to have been, in some degree, limited. Admitting that moderate and even well defined powers, long in the hands of the same man or family, will, probably, be unreasonably increased, it will not follow that even extensive powers placed in the hands of a man only for a few years will be abused. The Roman consuls and Carthagenian suffetes possessed extensive powers while in office; but being annually appointed, they but seldom, if ever, abused them. The Roman dictators often possessed absolute power while in office; but usually being elected for short periods of time, no one of them for ages usurped upon the rights of the people. The kings of France, Spain, Sweden, Denmark, &c. have become absolute merely from the encroachments and abuse of power made by the nobles. As to kings, and limited monarchs, generally, history furnishes many more instances in which their powers have been abridged or annihilated by the nobles or people, or both, than in which they have been increased or made absolute; and in almost all the latter cases we find the people were inattentive and fickle, and evidently were not born to be free. I am the more particular respecting this subject, because I have heard many mistaken observations relative to it.

Men

Men of property, and even men who hold powers for themfelves and posterity, have too much to lofe, wantonly to hazard a fhock of the political fyftem ; the game muft be large, and the chance of winning great, to induce them to rifque what they have, for the uncertain profpect of gaining more. Our executive may be altogether elective, and poffefs no power, but as the fubftitute of the people, and that well limited, and only for a limited time. The great object is, in a republican government, to guard effectually againft perpetuating any portion of power, great or fmall, in the fame man or family ; this perpetuation of power is totally uncongenial to the true fpirit of republican governments : on the one hand the firft executive magiftrate ought to remain in office fo long as to avoid inftability in the execution of the laws ; on the other, not fo long as to enable him to take any meafures to eftablifh himfelf. The convention, it feems, firft agreed that the prefident fhould be chofen for feven years, and never after to be eligible. Whether feven years is a period too long or not, is rather matter of opinion ; but clear it is, that this mode is infinitely preferable to the one finally adopted. When a man fhall get the chair, who may be re-elected, from time to time, for life, his greateft object will be to keep it ; to gain friends and votes, at any rate ; to affociate fome favourite fon with himfelf, to take the office after him : whenever he fhall have any profpect of continuing the office in himfelf and family, he will fpare no artifice, no addrefs, and no exertions, to increafe the powers and importance of it ; the fervile fupporters of his wifhes will be placed in all offices, and tools conftantly employed to aid his views and found his praife. A man fo fituated will have no permanent intereft in the government to lofe, by contefts and convulfions in the ftate, but always much to gain, and frequently the feducing and flattering hope of fucceeding. If we reafon at all on the fubject, we muft irrefiftably conclude, that this will be the cafe with nine tenths of the prefidents ; we may have, for the firft prefident, and, perhaps, one in a century or two afterwards (if the government fhould withftand the attacks of others)

a

a great and good man, governed by fuperior motives; but thefe are not events to be calculated upon in the prefent ftate of human nature.

A man chofen to this important office for a limited period, and always afterwards rendered, by the conftitution, ineligible, will be governed by very different confiderations: he can have no rational hopes or expectations of retaining his office after the expiration of a known limited time, or of continuing the office in his family, as by the conftitution there muft be a conftant transfer of it from one man to another, and confequently from one family to another. No man will wifh to be a mere cypher at the head of the government: the great object of each prefident then will be, to render his government a glorious period in the annals of his country. When a man conftitutionally retires from office, he retires without pain; he is fenfible he retires becaufe the laws direct it, and not from the fuccefs of his rivals, nor with that public difapprobation which being left out, when eligible, implies. It is faid, that a man knowing that at a given period he muft quit his office, will unjuftly attempt to take from the public, and lay in ftore the means of fupport and fplendour in his retirement; there can, I think, be but very little in this obfervation. The fame conftitution that makes a man eligible for a given period only, ought to make no man eligible till he arrive to the age of forty or forty-five years: if he be a man of fortune, he will retire with dignity to his eftate; if not, he may, like the Roman confuls, and other eminent characters in republics, find an honorable fupport and employment in fome refpectable office. A man who muft, at all events, thus leave his office, will have but few or no temptations to fill its dependant offices with his tools, or any particular fet of men; whereas the man conftantly looking forward to his future elections, and, perhaps, to the aggrandizement of his family, will have every inducement before him to fill all places with his own props and dependants. As to public monies, the prefident need handle none of them, and he may always rigidly be made account for every fhilling he fhall receive.

P 2

On

On the whole, it would be, in my opinion, almoſt as well to create a limited monarchy at once, and give ſome family permanent power and intereſt in the community, and let it have ſomething valuable to itſelf to loſe in convulſions in the ſtate, and in attempts of uſurpation, as to make a firſt magiſtrate eligible for life, and to create hopes and expectations in him and his family, of obtaining what they have not. In the latter caſe, we actually tempt them to diſturb the ſtate, to foment ſtruggles and conteſts, by laying before them the flattering proſpect of gaining much in them without riſking any thing.

The conſtitution provides only that the preſident ſhall hold his office during the term of four years; that, at moſt, only implies, that one ſhall be choſen every fourth year ; it alſo provides, that in caſe of the removal, death, reſignation, or inability, both of the preſident and vice-preſident, congreſs may declare what officer ſhall act as preſident ; and that ſuch officers ſhall act accordingly, until the diſability be removed, *or a preſident ſhall be elected*: it alſo provides that congreſs may determine the time of chuſing electors, and the day on which they ſhall give their votes. Conſidering theſe clauſes together, I ſubmit this queſtion—whether in caſe of a vacancy in the office of preſident, by the removal, death, reſignation, or inability of the preſident and vice-preſident, and congreſs ſhould declare, that a certain officer, as ſecretary for foreign affairs, for inſtance, ſhall act as preſident, and ſuffer ſuch officer to continue ſeveral years, or even for his life, to act as preſident, by omitting to appoint the time for chuſing electors of another preſident, it would be any breach of the conſtitution ? This appears to me to be an intended proviſion for ſupplying the office of preſident, not only for any remaining portion of the four years, but in caſes of emergency, until another preſident ſhall be elected ; and that at a period beyond the expiration of the four years : we do not know that it is impoſſible ; we do not know that it is improbable, in caſe a popular officer ſhould thus be declared the acting preſident, but that he might continue for life, and without any violent act,

act, but merely by neglects and delays on the part of congrefs.

I fhall conclude my obfervations on the organization of the legiflature and executive, with making fome re-marks, rather as a matter of amufement, on the branch, or partial negative, in the legiflation :—The third branch in the legiflature may anfwer three valuable purpofes, to impede in their paffage hafty and intemperate laws, occafionally to affift the fenate or people, and to pre-vent the legiflature from encroaching upon the executive or judiciary. In Great Britain the king has a complete negative upon all laws, but he very feldom exercifes it. This may be well lodged in him, who poffeffes ftrength to fupport it, and whofe family has independent and hereditary interefts and powers, rights and prerogatives, in the government, to defend : but in a country where the firft executive officer is elective, and has no rights, but in common with the people, a partial negative in legi-flation, as in Maffachufetts and New-York, is, in my opinion, clearly beft : in the former ftate, as before obferved, it is lodged in the governor alone ; in the latter, in the governor, chancellor, and judges of the fupreme court—the new conftitution lodges it in the prefident. This is fimply a branch of legiflative power, and has in itfelf no relation to executive or judicial powers. The queftion is, in what hands ought it to be lodged, to anfwer the three purpofes mentioned the moft advantageoufly ? The prevailing opinion feems to be in favour of vefting it in the hands of the firft execu-tive magiftrate. I will not fay this opinion is ill found-ed. The negative, in one cafe, is intended to prevent hafty laws, not fupported and revifed by two-thirds of each of the two braches ; in the fecond, it is to aid the weaker branch ; and in the third, to defend the execu-tive and judiciary. To anfwer thefe ends, there ought, therefore, to be collected in the hands which hold this negative, firmnefs, wifdom, and ftrength ; the very ob-ject of the negative is occafional oppofition to the two branches. By lodging it in the executive magiftrate, we give him a fhare in making the laws, which he muft execute ; by affociating the judges with him, as in

New-

New York, we give them a fhare in making the laws, upon which they muft decide as judicial magiftrates ; this may be a reafon for excluding the judges : however, the negative in New-York is certainly well calculated to anfwer its great purpofes : the governor and judges united muft poffefs more firmnefs and ftrength, more wifdom and information, than either alone, and alfo more of the confidence of the people ; and as to the balance among the departments, why fhould the executive alone hold the fcales, and the judicial be left defencelefs ? I think the negative in New-York is found beft in practice ; we fee it there frequently and wifely put upon the meafures of the two branches ; whereas in Maffachufetts it is hardly ever exercifed, and the governor, I believe, has often permitted laws to pafs to which he had fubftantial objections, but did not make them ; he, however, it is to be obferved, is annually elected.

The FEDERAL FARMER.

L E T T E R   XV.

January 18, 1788.

Dear Sir,

BEFORE I proceed to examine particularly the powers vefted, or which ought to be, vefted in each branch of the propofed government, I fhall briefly examine the organization of the remaining branch, the judicial, referring the particular examining of its powers to fome future letters.

In forming this branch, our objects are—a fair and open, a wife and impartial interpretation of the laws— a prompt and impartial adminiftration of juftice, between the public and individuals, and between man and man. I believe, there is no feature in a free government more difficult to be well formed than this, efpecially in an extenfive country, where the courts muft be numerous, or the citizens travel to obtain juftice,

The

The confederation impowers congrefs to inftitute judicial courts in four cafes. 1. For fettling difputes between individual ftates. 2. For determining, finally, appeals in all cafes of captures. 3. For the trial of piracies and felonies committed on the high feas: And, 4. For the adminiftration of martial law in the army and navy. The ftate courts in all other cafes poffefs the judicial powers, in all queftions arifing on the laws of nations, of the union, and of the ftates individually — nor does congrefs appear to have any controul over ftate courts, judges or officers. The bufinefs of the judicial department is, properly fpeaking, judicial in part, in part executive, done by judges and juries, by certain recording and executive officers, as clerks, fheriffs, &c. they are all properly limbs, or parts, of the judicial courts, and have it in charge, faithfully to decide upon, and execute the laws, in judicial cafes, between the public and individuals, between man and man. The recording and executive officers, in this department, may well enough be formed by legiflative acts, from time to time: but the offices, the fituation, the powers and duties of judges and juries, are too important, as they refpect the political fyftem, as well as the adminiftration of juftice, not to be fixed on general principles by the conftitution. It is true, the laws are made by the legiflature; but the judges and juries, in their interpretations, and in directing the execution of them, have a very extenfive influence for preferving or deftroying liberty, and for changing the nature of the government. It is an obfervation of an approved writer, that judicial power is of fuch a nature, that when we have afcertained and fixed its limits, with all the caution and precifion we can, it will yet be formidable, fomewhat arbitrary and defpotic—that is, after all our cares, we muft leave a vaft deal to the difcretion and interpretation—to the wifdom, integrity, and politics of the judges —Thefe men, fuch is the ftate even of the beft laws, may do wrong, perhaps, in a thoufand cafes, fometimes with, and fometimes without defign, yet it may be impracticable to convict them of mifconduct. Thefe confiderations fhew, how cautious a free people ought to be in forming this,

this, as well as the other branches of their government, especially when connected with other considerations equally deserving of notice and attention. When the legislature makes a bad law, or the first executive magistrates usurps upon the rights of the people, they discover the evil much sooner, than the abuses of power in the judicial department; the proceedings of which are far more intricate, complex, and out of their immediate view. A bad law immediately excites a general alarm; a bad judicial determination, though not less pernicious in its consequences, is immediately felt, probably, by a single individual only, and noticed only by his neighbours, and a few spectators in the court. In this country, we have been always jealous of the legislature, and especially the executive; but not always of the judiciary: but very few men attentively consider the essential parts of it, and its proceedings, as they tend to support or to destroy free government: only a few professional men are in a situation properly to do this; and it is often alledged, that instances have not frequently occurred, in which they have been found very alert watchmen in the cause of liberty, or in the cause of democratic republics. Add to these considerations, that particular circumstances exist at this time to increase our inattention to limiting properly the judicial powers, we may fairly conclude, we are more in danger of sowing the feeds of arbitrary government in this department than in any other. In the unsettled state of things in this country, for several years past, it has been thought, that our popular legislatures have, sometimes, departed from the line of strict justice, while the law courts have shewn a disposition more punctually to keep to it. We are not sufficiently attentive to the circumstances, that the measures of popular legislatures naturally settle down in time, and gradually approach a mild and just medium; while the rigid systems of the law courts naturally become more severe and arbitrary, if not carefully tempered and guarded by the constitution, and by laws, from time to time. It is true, much has been written and said about some of these courts lately, in some of the states; but all has been about their fees, &c. and

but

but very little to the purpofes, as to their influence upon
the freedom of the government.

By art. 3. fect. 1. the judicial power of the United
States fhall be vefted in one fupreme court, and in fuch
inferior courts, as congrefs may, from time to time,
ordain and eftablifh—the judges of them to hold their
offices during good behaviour, and to receive, at ftated
times, a compenfation for their fervices, which fhall not
be diminifhed during their continuance in office ; but
which, I conceive, may be increafed. By the fame art.
fect. 2. the fupreme court fhall have original jurifdiction,
" in all cafes affecting ambaffadors, and other public minifters, and confuls, and thofe in which a ftate fhall be
a party, and appellate jurifdiction, *both as to law and
fact*, in all other federal caufes, with fuch exceptions,
and under fuch regulations, as the congrefs fhall make."
By the fame fection, the judicial power fhall extend in
law and equity to all the federal cafes therein enumerated. By the fame fection the jury trial, in criminal
caufes, except in cafes of impeachment, is eftablifhed ;
but not in civil caufes, and the whole ftate may be confidered as the vicinage in cafes of crimes. Thefe claufes
prefent to view the conftitutional features of the federal
judieiary : this has been called a monfter by fome of
the opponents, and fome, even of the able advocates,
have confeffed they do not comprehend it. For myfelf,
I confefs, I fee fome good things in it, and fome very
extraordinary ones. " There fhall be one fupreme court."
There ought in every government to be one court, in
which all great queftions in law fhall finally meet and
be determined : in Great-Britain, this is the houfe of
lords, aided by all the fuperior judges ; in Maffachufetts, it is, at prefent, the fupreme judicial court, confifting of five judges ; in New-York, by the conftitution, it is a court confifting of the prefident of the fenate, the fenators, chancellor and judges of the fupreme
court ; and in the United States the federal fupreme
court, or this court in the laft refort, may, by the legiflature, be made to confift of three, five, fifty, or
any other number of judges. The inferior federal
courts are left by the conftitution to be inftituted and

Q   regulated

regulated altogether as the legiflature fhall judge beft;
and it is well provided, that the judges fhall hold their
offices during good behaviour. I fhall not objeƈt to
the line drawn between the original and appellate jurifdiƈtion of the fupreme court ; though fhould we for
fafety, &c. be obliged to form a numerous fupreme
court, and place in it a confiderable number of refpectable charaƈters, it will be found inconvenient for fuch
a court, originally, to try all the caufes affeƈting ambaffadors, confuls, &c. Appeals may be carried up to
the fupreme court, under fuch regulations as congrefs
fhall make. Thus far the legiflature does not appear
to be limited to improper rules or principles in inftituting judicial courts : indeed the legiflature will have
full power to form and arrange judicial courts in the
federal cafes enumerated, at pleafure, with thefe eight
exceptions only. 1. There can be but one fupreme federal judicial court. 2. This muft have jurifdiƈtion as
to law and faƈt in the appellate caufes. 3. Original
jurifdiƈtion, when foreign minifters and the ftates are
concerned. 4. The judges of the judicial courts muft
continue in office during good behaviour—and, 5.Their
falaries cannot be diminifhed while in office. 6. There
muft be a jury trial in criminal caufes. 7. The trial of
crimes muft be in the ftate where committed—and, 8.
There muft be two witneffes to conviƈt of treafon.

In all other refpeƈts Congrefs may organize the judicial department according to their difcretion ; the importance of this power, among others propofed by the
legiflature (perhaps neceffarily) I fhall confider hereafter. Though there muft, by the conftitution, be but
one judicial court, in which all the rays of judicial powers as to law, equity, and faƈt, in the cafes enumerated
muft meet ; yet this may be made by the legiflature, a
fpecial court, confifting of any number of refpeƈtable
charaƈters or officers, the federal legiflators excepted, to fuperintend the judicial department, to try the
few caufes in which foreign minifters and the ftates may
be concerned, and to correƈt errors,as to law and faƈt, in
certain important caufes on appeals. Next below this
judicial head, there may be feveral courts, fuch as are
ufually

ufually called fuperior courts, as a court of chancery, a court of criminal jurifdiction, a court of civil jurifdiction, a court of admiralty jurifdiction, a court of exchequer, &c. giving an appeal from thefe refpectively to the fupreme judicial court. Thefe fuperior courts may be confidered as fo many points to which appeals may be brought up, from the varions inferior courts, in the feveral branches of judicial caufes. In all thefe fuperior and inferior courts, the trial by jury may be eftablifhed in all cafes, and the law and equity properly feparated. In this organization, only a few very important caufes, probably, would be carried up to the fupreme court.— The fuperior courts would, finally, fettle almoft all caufes. This organization, fo far as it would refpect queftions of law, inferior, fuperior, and a fpecial fupreme court, would refemble that of New-York in a confiderable degree, and thofe of feveral other ftates. This, I imagine, we muft adopt, or elfe the Maffachufetts plan ; that is, a number of inferior courts, and one fuperior or fupreme court, confifting of three, or five, or feven judges, in which one fupreme court all the bufinefs fhall be immediately collected from the inferior ones. The decifion of the inferior courts, on either plan, probably will not much be relied on ; and on the latter plan, there muft be a prodigious accumulation of powers and bufinefs in all cafes touching law, equity and facts, and all kinds of caufes in a few hands, for whofe errors of ignorance or defign, there will be no poffible remedy. As the legiflature may adopt either of thefe, or any other plan, I fhall not dwell longer on this fubject.

In examining the federal judiciary, there appears to be fome things very extraordinary and very peculiar. The judges or their friends may feize every opportunity to raife the judges falaries ; but by the conftitution they cannot be diminifhed. I am fenfible how important it is that judges fhall always have adequate and certain fupport ; I am againft their depending upon annual or periodical grants, becaufe thefe may be withheld, or rendered too fmall by the diffent or narrownefs of any one branch of the legiflature ; but there is a material diftinction between periodical grants, and falaries

laries held under permanent and standing laws : the former at stated periods cease, and must be renewed by the consent of all and every part of the legislature , the latter continue of course, and never will cease or be lowered, unless all parts of the legislature agree to do it. A man has as permanent an interest in his salary fixed by a standing law, so long as he may remain in office, as in any property he may possess ; for the laws regulating the tenure of all property, are always liable to be altered by the legislature. The same judge may frequently be in office thirty or forty years ; there may often be times, as in cases of war, or very high prices, when his salary may reasonably be increased one half or more ; in a few years money may become scarce again, and prices fall, and his salary, with equal reason and propriety be decreased and lowered : not to suffer this to be done by consent of all the branches of the legislature, is, I believe, quite a novelty in the affairs of government. It is true, by a very forced and unnatural construction, the constitution of Massachusetts, by the governor and minority in the legislature, was made to speak this kind of language. Another circumstance ought to be considered ; the mines which have been discovered are gradually exhausted, and the precious metals are continually wasting : hence the probability is, that money, the nominal representative of property, will gradually grow scarcer hereafter, and afford just reasons for gradually lowering salaries. The value of money depends altogether upon the quantity of it in circulation, which may be also decreased, as well as encreased, from a great variety of causes.

The supreme court, in cases of appeals, shall have jurisdiction both as to law and fact : that is, in all civil causes carried up the supreme court by appeals, the court, or judges, shall try the fact and decide the law. Here an essential principle of the civil law is established, and the most noble and important principle of the common law exploded. To dwell a few minutes on this material point : the supreme court shall have jurisdiction both as to law and fact. What is meant by court ? Is the jury included in the term, or is it not ?

I

I conceive it is not included : and so the members of convention, I am very sure, understand it. Court, or curia, was a term well understood long before juries exifted ; the people, and the best writers, in countries where there are no juries, uniformly use the word court, and can only mean by it the judge or judges who determine causes : also, in countries where there are juries we express ourselves in the same manner ; we speak of the court of probate, court of chancery, justices court, alderman's court, &c. in which there is no jury. In our supreme courts, common pleas, &c. in which there are jury trials, we uniformly speak of the court and jury, and confider them as distinct. Were it necessary I might site a multitude of cases from law books to confirm, beyond controversy, this position, that the jury is not included, or a part of the court.

But the supreme court is to have jurisdiction as to law and fact, under such regulations as congress shall make. I confess it is impossible to say how far congress may, with propriety, extend their regulations in this respect. I conceive, however, they cannot by any reasonable construction go so far as to admit the jury, on true common law principles, to try the fact, and give a general verdict. I have repeatedly examined this article : I think the meaning of it is, that the judges in all final questions, as to property and damages, shall have complete jurisdiction, to consider the whole cause, to examine the facts, and on a general view of them, and on principles of equity, as well as law, to give judgment.

As the trial by jury is provided for in criminal causes, I shall confine my obfervations to civil causes—and in thefe, I hold it is the eftablished right of the jury by the common law, and the fundamental laws of this country, to give a general verdict in all cases when they chufe to do it, to decide both as to law and fact, whenever blended together in the iffue put to them. Their right to determine as to facts will not be difputed, and their right to give a general verdict has never been difputed, except by a few judges and lawyers, governed by defpotic principles. Coke, Hale, Holt, Blackftone, De
R
Lome,

Lome, and almoſt every other legal or political writer,
who has written on the ſubjeƈt, has uniformly aſſerted
this eſſential and important right of the jury. Juries
in Great-Britain and America have univerſally praƈtiſed
accordingly. Even Mansfield, with all his wiſhes about
him, dare not direƈtly avow the contrary. What fully
confirms this point is, that there is no inſtance to be
found, where a jury was ever puniſhed for finding a
general verdiƈt, when a ſpecial one might, with propriety, have been found. The jury trial, eſpecially
politically confidered, is by far the moſt important feature in the judicial department in a free country, and the
right in queſtion is far the moſt valuable part, and the
laſt that ought to be yielded, of this trial. Juries are
conſtantly and frequently drawn from the body of the
people, and freemen of the country ; and by holding
the jury's right to return a general verdiƈt in all caſes
ſacred, we ſecure to the people at large, their juſt and
rightful controul in the judicial department. If the
conduƈt of judges ſhall be ſevere and arbitrary, and
tend to ſubvert the the laws, and change the forms of
government, the jury may check them, by deciding
againſt their opinions and determinations, in ſimilar
caſes. It is true, the freemen of a country are not
always minutely ſkilled in the laws, but they have common ſenſe in its purity, which ſeldom or never errs in
making and applying laws to the condition of the people, or in determining judicial cauſes, when ſtated to
them by the parties. The body of the people, principally, bear the burdens of the community ; they of
right ought to have a controul in its important concerns, both in making and executing the laws, other-
wiſe they may, in a ſhort time, be ruined. Nor is it
merely this controul alone we are to attend to : the
jury trial brings with it an open and public diſcuſſion
of all cauſes, and excludes ſecret and arbitrary proceedings. This, and the democratic branch in the legiſlature, as was formerly obſerved, are the means by which
the people are let into the knowledge of public affairs—
are enabled to ſtand as the guardians of each others
rights, and to reſtrain, by regular and legal meaſures,
thoſe

thofe who otherwife might infringe upon them. I am
not unfupported in my opinion of the value of the trial
by jury ; not only Britifh and American writers, but De
Lome, and the moft approved foreign writers, hold it
to be the moft valuable part of the Britifh conflitution,
and indifputably the beft mode of trial ever invented.

It was merely by the intrigues of the popifh clergy,
and of the Norman lawyers, that this mode of trial was
not ufed in maritime, ecclefiaftical, and military courts,
and the civil law proceedings were introduced ; and, I
believe, it is more from cuftom and prejudice, than for
any fubftantial reafons, that we do not in all the ftates
eftablifh the jury in our maritime as well as other
courts.

In the civil law procefs the trial by jury is unknown ;
the confequence is, that a few judges and dependant
officers, poffefs all the power in the judicial department.
Inftead of the open fair proceedings of the common law,
where witneffes are examined in open court, and may be
crofs examined by the parties concerned—where council
is allowed, &c. we fee in the civil law procefs judges
alone, who always, long previous to the trial, are known
and often corrupted by minifterial influence, or by parties. Judges once influenced, foon become inclined to
yield to temptations, and to decree for him who will
pay the moft for their partiality. It is, therefore, we
find in the Roman, and almoft all governments, where
judges alone poffefs the judicial powers and try all cafes,
that bribery has prevailed. This, as well as the forms
of the courts, naturally lead to fecret and arbitrary proceedings—to taking evidence fecretly—exparte, &c.
to perplexing the caufe—and to hafty decifions :—but,
as to jurors, it is quite impracticable to bribe or influence them by any corrupt means ; not only becaufe
they are untaught in fuch affairs, and poffefs the honeft
characters of the common freemen of a country ; but
becaufe it is not, generally, known till the hour the
caufe comes on for trial, what perfons are to form the
jury.

But it is faid, that no words could be found by which
the ftates could agree to eftablifh the jury-trial in civil

R 2   caufes.

caufes. I can hardly believe men to be ferious, who make obfervations to this effect. The ftates have all derived judicial proceedings principally from one fource, the Britifh fyftem ; from the fame common fource the American lawyers have almoft univerfally drawn their legal information. All the ftates have agreed to efta-blifh the trial by jury, in civil as well as in criminal caufes. The feveral ftates, in congrefs, found no diffi-culty in eftablifhing it in the Weftern Territory, in the ordinance paffed in July 1787. We find, that the feve-ral ftates in congrefs, in eftablifhing government in that territory, agreed, that the inhabitants of it, fhould al-ways be entitled to the benefit of the trial by jury. Thus, in a few words, the jury trial is eftablifhed in its full extent ; and the convention with as much eafe, have eftablifhed the jury trial in criminal cafes. In making a conftitution, we are fubftantially to fix principles.— If in one ftate, damages on default are affeffed by a ju-ry, and in another by the judges—if in one ftate jurors are drawn out of a box, and in another not—if there be other trifling variations, they can be of no impor-tance in the great queftion. Further, when we examine the particular practices of the ftates, in little matters in judicial proceedings, I believe we fhall find they dif-fer near as much in criminal proceffes as in civil ones. Another thing worthy of notice in this place—the con-vention have ufed the word equity, and agreed to efta-blifh a chancery jurifdiction ; about the meaning and extent of which, we all know, the feveral ftates dif-agree much more than about jury trials—in adopting the latter, they have very generally purfued the Britifh plan ; but as to the former, we fee the ftates have varied, as their fears and opinions dictated.

By the common law, in Great Britain and America, there is no appeal from the verdict of the jury, as to facts, to any judges whatever—the jurifdiction of the jury is complete and final in this ; and only errors in law are carried up to the houfe of lords, the fpecial fupreme court in Great Britain ; or to the fpecial fupreme courts in Connecticut, New-York, New-Jerfey, &c. Thus the juries are left mafters as to facts: but,
by

by the propofed conftitution, directly the oppofite principles is eftablifhed. An appeal will lay in all appellate caufes from the verdict of the jury, even as to mere
facts, to the judges of the fupreme court. Thus, in
effect, we eftablifh the civil law in this point; for if the
jurifdiction of the jury be not final, as to facts, it is of
little or no importance.

By art. 3. fect. 2. " the judicial power fhall extend to
all cafes in law and equity, arifing under this conftitution, the laws of the United States," &c. What is here
meant by equity? what is equity in a cafe arifing under
the conftitution? poffibly the claufe might have the fame
meaning, were the words " in law and equity," omitted.
Cafes in law muft differ widely from cafes in law and
equity. At firft view, by thus joining the word equity
with the word law, if we mean any thing, we feem to
mean to give the judge a difcretionary power. The
word equity, in Great Britain, has in time acquired a
precife meaning—chancery proceedings there are now
reduced to fyftem—but this is not the cafe in the
United States. In New-England, the judicial courts
have no powers in cafes in equity, except thofe dealt
out to them by the legiflature, in certain limited por-
tions, by legiflative acts. In New-York, Maryland,
Virginia, and South-Carolina, powers to decide, in cafes
of equity, are vefted in judges diftinct from thofe who
decide in matters of law: and the ftates generally feem
to have carefully avoided giving unlimitedly, to the fame
judges, powers to decide in cafes in law and equity.
Perhaps, the claufe would have the fame meaning were
the words, " this conftitution," omitted: there is in it
either a carelefs complex mifufe of words, in themfelves
of extenfive fignification, or there is fome meaning not
eafy to be comprehended. Suppofe a cafe arifing under
the conftitution—fuppofe the queftion judicially moved,
whether, by the conftitution, congrefs can fupprefs a
ftate tax laid on polls, lands, or as an excife duty,
which may be fuppofed to interfere with a federal tax.
By the letter of the conftitution, congrefs will appear to
have no power to do it: but then the judges may decide the queftion on principles of equity as well as law.

Now,

Now, omitting the words, "in law and equity," they may decide according to the fpirit and true meaning of the conftitution, as collected from what muft appear to have been the intentions of the people when they made it. Therefore, it would feem, that if thefe words mean any thing, they muft have a further meaning : yet I will not fuppofe it intended to lodge an arbitrary power or difcretion in the judges, to decide as their confcience, their opinions, their caprice, or their politics might dictate. Without dwelling on this obfcure claufe, I will leave it to the examination of others.

THE FEDERAL FARMER.

L E T T E R   XVI.

JANUARY 20, 1788.

DEAR SIR,

HAVING gone through with the organization of the government, I fhall now proceed to examine more particularly thofe claufes which refpect its powers. I fhall begin with thofe articles and ftipulations which are neceffary for accurately afcertaining the extent of powers, and what is given, and for guarding limiting, and reftraining them in their exercife. We often find, thefe articles and ftipulations placed in bills of rights ; but they may as well be incorporated in the body of the conftitution, as felected and placed by themfelves. The conftitution, or whole focial compact, is but one inftrument, no more or lefs, than a certain number of articles or ftipulations agreed to by the people, whether it confifts of articles, fections, chapters, bills of rights, or parts of any other denomination, cannot be material. Many needlefs obfervations, and idle diftinctions, in my opinion, have been made refpecting a bill of rights. On the one hand, it feems to be confidered as a neceffary diftinct limb of the conftitution, and as containing a certain number of very valuable articles, which are applicable to all focieties : and, on the other, as ufelefs,

efpecially

efpecially in a federal government, poffeffing only enumerated power--nay, dangerous, as individual rights are
numerous, and not eafy to be enumerated in a bill of
rights, and from articles, or ftipulations, fecuring fome
of them, it may be inferred, that others not mentioned
are furrendered. There appears to me to be general
indefinite propofitions without much meaning—and the
man who firft advanced thofe of the latter defcription,
in the prefent cafe, figned the federal conftitution,
which directly contradicts him. The fupreme power is
undoubtedly in the people, and it is a principle well
eftablifhed in my mind, that they referve all powers not
exprefsly delegated by them to thofe who govern ; this
is as true in forming a ftate as in forming a federal government. There is no poffible diftinction but this
founded merely in the different modes of proceeding
which take place in fome cafes. In forming a ftate
conftitution, under which to manage not only the great
but the little concerns of a community : the powers
to be poffeffed by the government are often too numerous to be enumerated ; the people to adopt the fhorteft
way often give general powers, indeed all powers, to
the government, in fome general words, and then, by
a particular enumeration, take back, or rather fay they
however referve certain rights as facred, and which no
laws fhall be made to violate : hence the idea that all
powers are given which are not referved : but in forming a federal conftitution, which *ex vi termine*, fuppofes
ftate governments exifting, and which is only to manage
a few great national concerns, we often find it eafier to
enumerate particularly the powers to be delegated to
the federal head, than to enumerate particularly the individual rights to be referved ; and the principle will
operate in its full force, when we carefully adhere to it.
When we particularly enumerate the powers given, we
ought either carefully to enumerate the rights referved,
or be totally filent about them ; we muft either particularly enumerate both, or elfe fuppofe the particular
enumeration of the powers given adequately draws the
line between them and the rights referved, particularly
to enumerate the former and not the latter, I think moft
advifable

advifable : however, as men appear generally to have
their doubts about thefe filent refervations, we might
advantageoufly enumerate the powers given, and then
in general words, according to the mode adopted in the
2d art. of the confederation, declare all powers, rights
and privileges, are referved, which are not explicitly
and exprefsly given up. People, and very wifely too,
like to be exprefs and explicit about their effential rights,
and not to be forced to claim them on the precarious
and unafcertained tenure of inferences and general principles, knowing that in any controverfy between them
and their rulers, concerning thofe rights, ; difputes
may be endlefs, and nothing certain :—But admitting,
on the general principle, that all rights are referved of
courfe, which are not exprefsly furrendered, the people could with fufficient certainty affert their rights
on all occafions, and eftablifh them with eafe, ftill there
are infinite advantages in particularly enumerating many
of the moft effential rights referved in all cafes ; and as
to the lefs important ones, we may declare in general
terms, that all not exprefsly furrendered are referved.
We do not by declarations change the nature of things,
or create new truths, but we give exiftence, or at leaft
eftablifh in the minds of the people truths and principles which they might never otherwife have thought of,
or foon forgot. If a nation means its fyftems, religious
or political, fhall have duration, it ought to recognize
the leading principles of them in the front page of every
family book. What is the ufefulnefs of a truth in
theory, unlefs it exifts conftantly in the minds of the
people, and has their affent :—we difcern certain rights,
as the freedom of the prefs, and the trial by jury, &c.
which the people of England and of America of courfe
believe to be facred, and effential to their political happinefs, and this belief in them is the refult of ideas at
firft fuggefted to them by a few able men, and of fubfequent experience ; while the people of fome other
countries hear thefe rights mentioned with the utmoft
indifference ; they think the privilege of exifting at the
will of a defpot much preferable to them. Why this
difference amongft beings every way formed alike.
The

The reason of the difference is obvious—it is the effect of education, a series of notions impressed upon the minds of the people by examples, precepts and declarations. When the people of England got together, at the time they formed Magna Charta, they did not consider it sufficient, that they were indisputably entitled to certain natural and unalienable rights, not depending on silent titles, they, by a declaratory act, expressly recognized them, and explicitly declared to all the world, that they were entitled to enjoy those rights ; they made an instrument in writing, and enumerated those they then thought essential, or in danger, and this wise men saw was not sufficient ; and therefore, that the people might not forget these rights, and gradually become prepared for arbitrary government, their discerning and honest leaders caused this instrument to be confirmed near forty times, and to be read twice a year in public places, not that it would lose its validity without such confirmations, but to fix the contents of it in the minds of the people, as they successively come upon the stage.——Men, in some countries do not remain free, merely because they are entitled to natural and unalienable rights ; men in all countries are entitled to them, not because their ancestors once got together and enumerated them on paper, but because, by repeated negociations and declarations, all parties are brought to realize them, and of course to believe them to be sacred. Were it necessary, I might shew the wisdom of our past conduct, as a people in not merely comforting ourselves that we were entitled to freedom, but in constantly keeping in view, in addresses, bills of rights, in news-papers, &c. the particular principles on which our freedom must always depend.

It is not merely in this point of view, that I urge the engrafting in the constitution additional declaratory articles. The distinction, in itself just, that all powers not given are reserved, is in effect destroyed by this very constitution, as I shall particularly demonstrate—and even independent of this, the people, by adopting the constitution, give many general undefined powers to

S   congress, congrefs, in the conftitutianal exercife of which, the rights in queftion may be effected. Gentlemen who oppofe a federal bill of rights, or further declaratory articles, feem to view the fubject in a very narrow imperfect manner. Thefe have for their objects, not only the enumeration of the rights referved, but principally to explain the general powers delegated in certain material points, and to reftrain thofe who exercife them by fixed known boundaries. Many explanations and reftrictions neceffary and ufeful, would be much lefs fo, were the people at large all well and fully acquainted with the principles and affairs of government. There appears to be in the conftitution, a ftudied brevity, and it may alfo be probable, that feveral explanatory articles were omitted from a circumftance very common. What we have long and early underftood ourfelves in the common concerns of the community, we are apt to fuppofe is underftood by others, and need not be expreffed ; and it is not unnatural or uncommon for the ableft men moft frequently to make this miftake. To make declaratory articles unneceffary in an inftrument of government, two circumftances muft exift ; the rights referved muft be indifputably fo, and in their nature defined ; the powers delegated to the government, muft be precifely defined by the words that convey them, and clearly be of fuch extent and nature as that, by no reafonble conftruction, they can be made to invade the rights and prerogatives intended to be left in the people.

The firft point urged, is, that all power is referved not exprefsly given, that particular enumerated powers only are given, that all others are not given, but referved, and that it is needlefs to attempt to reftrain congrefs in the exercife of powers they poffefs not. This reafoning is logical, but of very little importance in the common affairs of men ; but the conftitution does not appear to refpect it even in any view. To prove this, I might cite feveral claufes in it. I fhall only remark on two or three. By article 1, fection 9, " No title of nobility fhall be granted by congrefs." Was this claufe omitted, what power would congrefs have to make titles of nobility ? in what part of the conftitution would
they

they find it ? The anfwer muft be, that congrefs would have no fuch power—that the people, by adopting the conftitution, will not part with it. Why then by a negative claufe, reftrain congrefs from doing what it would have no power to do ? This claufe, then, muft have no meaning, or imply, that were it omitted, congrefs would have the power in queftion, either upon the principle that fome general words in the conftitution may be fo conftrued as to give it, or on the principle that congrefs poffefs the powers not exprefsly referved. But this claufe was in the confederation, and is faid to be introduced into the conftitution from very great caution. Even a cautionary provifion implies a doubt, at leaft, that it is neceffary ; and if fo in this cafe, clearly it is alfo alike neceffary in all fimilar ones. The fact appears to be, that the people in forming the confederation, and the convention, in this inftance, acted, naturally, they did not leave the point to be fettled by general principles and logical inferences ; but they fettle the point in a few words, and all who read them at once underftand them.

The trial by jury in criminal as well as in civil caufes, has long been confidered as one of our fundamental rights, and has been repeatedly recognized and confirmed by moft of the ftate conventions. But the conftitution exprefsly eftablifhes this trial in criminal, and wholly omits it in civil caufes. The jury trial in criminal caufes, and the benefit of the writ of habeas corpus, are already as effectually eftablifhed as any of the fundamental or effential rights of the people in the United States. This being the cafe, why in adopting a federal conftitution do we now eftablifh thefe, and omit all others, or all others, at leaft with a few exceptions, fuch as again agreeing there fhall be no ex poft facto laws, no titles of nobility, &c. We muft confider this conftitution, when adopted, as the fupreme act of the people, and in conftruing it hereafter, we and our pofterity muft ftrictly adhere to the letter and fpirit of it, and in no inftance depart from them : in conftruing the federal conftitution, it will be not only impracticable, but improper to refer to the ftate conftitutions. They are entirely

tirely diftinct inftruments and inferior acts : befides, by
the people's now eftablifhing certain fundamental rights,
it is ftrongly implied, that they are of opinion, that
they would not otherwife be, fecured as a part of the
federal fyftem, or be regarded in the federal adminiftration as fundamental.   Further, thefe fame rights, being
eftablifhed by the ftate conftitutions, and fecured to the
people, our recognizing them now, implies, that the
people thought them infecure by the ftate eftablifhments, and extinguifhed or put afloat by the new arrangement of the focial fyftem, unlefs re-eftablifhed. —
Further, the people, thus eftablifhing fome few rights,
and remaining totally filent about others fimilarly circumftanced, the implication indubitably is, that they
mean to relinquifh the latter or at leaft feel indifferent
about them.   Rights, therefore, inferred from general
principles of reafon, being precarious and hardly afcer-
tainable in the common affairs of fociety, and the people, in forming a federal conftitution, explicitly fhewing
they conceive thefe rights to be thus circumftanced, and
accordingly proceed to enumerate and eftablifh fome of
them, the conclufion will be, that they have eftablifhed
all which they efteem valuable and facred.   On every
principle, then, the people efpecially having began,
ought to go through enumerating, and eftablifh particularly all the rights of individuals, which can by any
poffibility come in queftion in making and executing
federal laws.   I have already obferved upon the excel-
lency and importance of the jury trial in civil as well
as in criminal caufes, inftead of eftablifhing it in criminal caufes only ; we ought to eftablifh it generally ;—
inftead of the claufe of forty or fifty words relative to
this fubject, why not ufe the language that has always
been ufed in this country, and fay, " the people of the
United States fhall always be entitled to the trial by jury."   This would fhew the people ftill hold the right
facred, and enjoin it upon congrefs fubftantially to preferve the jury trial in all cafes, according to the ufage
and cuftom of the country.   I have obferved before,
that it is *the jury trial* we want ; the little different appendages and modifications tacked to it in the different
fstate

ftates, are no more than a drop in the ocean : the jury trial is a folid uniform feature in a free government ; it is the fubftance we would fave, not the little articles of form.

Security againft expoft facto laws, the trial by jury, and the benefits of the writ of habeas corpus, are but a part of thofe ineftimable rights the people of the United States are entitled to, even in judicial proceedings, by the courfe of the common law. Thefe may be fecured in general words, as in New-York, the Weftern Territory, &c. by declaring the people of the United States fhall always be entitled to judicial proceedings according to the courfe of the common law, as ufed and eftablifhed in the faid ftates. Perhaps it would be better to enumerate the particular effential rights the people are entitled to in thefe proceedings, as has been done in many of the ftates, and as has been done in England. In this cafe, the people may proceed to declare, that no man fhall be held to anfwer to any offence, till the fame be fully defcribed to him ; nor to furnifh evidence againft himfelf : that, except in the government of the army and navy, no perfon fhall be tried for any offence, whereby he may incur lofs of life, or an infamous punifhment, until he be firft indicted by a grand jury : that every perfon fhall have a right to produce all proofs that may be favourable to him, and to meet the witneffes againft him face to face : that every perfon fhall be entitled to obtain right and juftice freely and without delay : that all perfons fhall have a right to be fecure from all unreafonable fearches and feizures of their perfons, houfes, papers, or poffeffions ; and that all warrants fhall be deemed contrary to this right, if the foundation of them be not previoufly fupported by oath, and there be not in them a fpecial defignation of perfons or objects of fearch, arreft, or feizure : and that no perfon fhall be exiled or molefted in his perfon or effects, otherwife than by the judgment of his peers, or according to the law of the land. A celebrated writer obferves upon this laft article, that in itfelf it may be faid to comprehend the whole end of political fociety. Thefe rights are not neceffarily referved, they are eftablifhed, or en-

T   joyed

joyed but in few countries: they are ftipulated rights, almoft peculiar to Britifh and American laws. In the execution of thofe laws, individuals, by long cuftom, by magna charta, bills of rights &c. have become entitled to them. A man, at firft, by act of parliament, became entitled to the benefits of the writ of habeas corpus—men are entitled to thefe rights and benefits in the judicial proceedings of our ftate courts generally : but it will by no means follow, that they will be entitled to them in the federal courts, and have a right to affert them, unlefs fecured and eftablifhed by the conftitution or federal laws. We certainly, in federal procefles, might as well claim the benefits of the writ of habeas corpus, as to claim trial by a jury--the right to have council—to have witnefles face to face—to be fecure againft unreafonable fearch warrants, &c. was the conftitution filent as to the whole of them :—but the eftablifhment of the former, will evince that we could not claim them without it ; and the omiffion of the latter, implies they are relinquifhed, or deemed of no importance. Thefe are rights and benefits individuals acquire by compact ; they muft claim them under compacts, or immemorial ufage—it is doubtful, at leaft, whether they can be claimed under immemorial ufage in this country ; and it is, therefore, we generally claim them under compacts, as charters and conftitutions.

The people by adopting the federal conftitution, give congrefs general powers to inftitute a diftinct and new judiciary, new courts, and to regulate all proceedings in them, under the eight limitations mentioned in a former letter ; and the further one, that the benefits of the habeas corpus act fhall be enjoyed by individuals. Thus general powers being given to inftitute courts, and regulate their proceedings, with no provifion for fecuring the rights principally in queftion, may not congrefs fo exercife thofe powers, and conftitutionally too, as to deftroy thofe rights ? clearly, in my opinion, they are not in any degree fecured. But, admitting the cafe is only doubtful, would it not be prudent and wife to fecure them and remove all doubts, fince all agree the people ought to enjoy thefe valuable rights, a very few

men

men excepted, who feem to be rather of opinion that there is little or nothing in them ? Were it neceffary I might add many obfervations to fhew their value and political importance.

The conftitution will give congrefs general powers to raife and fupport armies. General powers carry with them incidental ones, and the means neceffary to the end. In the exercife of thefe powers, is there any provifion in the conftitution to prevent the quartering of folciers on the inhabitants ? you will anfwer, there is not. This may fometimes be deemed a neceffary meafure in the fupport of armies ; on what principle can the people claim the right to be exempt from this burden ? they will urge, perhaps, the practice of the country, and the provifions made in fome of the ftate conftitutions—they will be anfwered, that their claim thus to be exempt is not founded in nature, but only in cuftom and opinicn, or at beft, in ftipulations in fome of the ftate conftitutions, which are local, and inferior in their operation, and can have no controul over the general government —that they had adopted a federal conftitution—had noticed feveral rights, but had been totally filent about this exemption—that they had given general powers relative to the fubject, which, in their operation. regularly deftroyed the claim. Though it is not to be prefumed, that we are in any immediate danger from this quarter, yet it is fit and proper to eftablifh, beyond difpute, thofe rights which are particularly valuable to individuals, and effential to the permanency and duration of free government. An excellent writer obferves, that the Englifh, always in poffeffion of their freedom, are frequently unmindful of the value of it: we, at this period, do not feem to be fo well off, having, in fome inftances abufed ours ; many of us are quite difpofed to barter it away for what we call energy, coercion, and fome other terms we ufe as vaguely as that of liberty——There is often as great a rage for change and novelty in politics, as in amufements and fafhions.

All parties apparently agree, that the freedom of the prefs is a fundamental right, and ought not to be reftrained by any taxes, duties, or in any manner whatever.

Why

Why fhould not the people, in adopting a federal conftitution, declare this, even if there are only doubts
about it. But, fay the advocates, all powers not given
are referved :—true ; but the great queftion is, are not
powers given, in the excercife of which this right may
be deftroyed ? The people's or the printers claim to a
free prefs, is founded on the fundamental laws, that is,
compacts, and ftate conftitutions, made by the people.
The people, who can annihilate or alter thofe conftitutions, can annihilate or limit this right. This may be
done by giving general powers, as well as by ufing particular words. No right claimed under a ftate conftitution, will avail againft a law of the union, made in
purfuance of the federal conftitution : therefore the
queftion is, what laws will congrefs have a right to make
by the conftitution of the union, and particularly touching the prefs ? By art. 1. fect. 8. congrefs will have
power to lay and collect taxes, duties, impofts and
excife. By this congrefs will clearly have power to lay
and collect all kind of taxes whatever—taxes on houfes,
lands, polls, induftry, merchandize, &c.—taxes on deeds,
bonds, and all written inftruments—on writs, pleas, and
all judicial proceedings, on licences, naval officers papers, &c. on newfpapers, advertifements, &c. and to
require bonds of the naval officers, clerks, printers, &c.
to account for the taxes that may become due on papers
that go through their hands. Printing, like all other
bufinefs, muft ceafe when taxed beyond its profits ; and
it appears to me, that a power to tax the prefs at difcretion, is a power to deftroy or reftrain the freedom of it.
There may be other powers given, in the exercife of
which this freedom may be effected; and certainly it is
of too much importance to be left thus liable to be taxed, and conftantly to conftructions and inferences. A
free prefs is the channel of communication as to mercantile and public affairs ; by means of it the people in
large countries afcertain each others fentiments ; are
enabled to unite, and become formidable to thofe rulers
who adopt improper meafures. Newfpapers may fometimes be the vehicles of abufe, and of many things not
true ; but thefe are but fmall inconveniencies, in my
mind,

mind, among many advantages. A celebrated writer, I have several times quoted, speaking in high terms of the English liberties, says, " lastly the key stone was put to the arch, by the final establishment of the freedom of the press." I shall not dwell longer upon the funda. mental rights, to some of which I have attended in this letter, for the same reasons that these I have mentioned, ought to be expressly secured, left in the exercise of general powers given they may be invaded: it is pretty clear, that some other of less importance, or less in danger, might with propriety also be secured.

I shall now proceed to examine briefly the powers proposed to be vested in the several branches of the government, and especially the mode of laying and collecting internal taxes.

THE FEDERAL FARMER.

LETTER XVII.

JANUARY 23, 1788.

DEAR SIR,

I BELIEVE the people of the United States are full in the opinion, that a free and mild government can be preserved in their extensive territories, only under the substantial forms of a federal republic. As several of the ablest advocates for the system proposed, have acknowledged this (and I hope the confessions they have published will be preserved and remembered) I shall not take up time to establish this point. A question then arises, how far that system partakes of a federal republic.—I observed in a former letter, that it appears to be the first important step to a consolidation of the states; that its strong tendency is to that point.

But what do we mean by a federal republic? and what by a consolidated government? To erect a federal republic, we must first make a number of states on republican principles; each state with a government organized for the internal management of its affairs: The

states,

ſtates, as ſuch, muſt unite under a federal head, and delegate to it powers to make and execute laws in certain
enumerated caſes, under certain reſtrictions; this head
may be a ſingle aſſembly, like the preſent congreſs, or
the Amphictionic council ; or it may conſiſt of a legiſlature, with one or more branches ; of an executive, and
of a judiciary. To form a conſolidated, or one entire
government, there muſt be no ſtate, or local governments, but all things, perſons and property, muſt be
ſubject to the laws of one legiſlature alone ; to one executive, and one judiciary. Each ſtate government, as
the government of New jerſey, &c. is a conſolidated, or
one entire government, as it reſpects the counties, towns,
citizens and property within the limits of the ſtate.——
The ſtate governments are the baſis, the pillar on which
the federal head is placed, and the whole together, when
formed on elective principles, conſtitute a federal republic. A federal republic in itſelf ſuppoſes ſtate or local
governments to exiſt, as the body or props, on which
the federal head reſts, and that it cannot remain a moment after they ceaſe. In erecting the federal government, and always in its councils, each ſtate muſt be
known as a ſovereign body ; but in erecting this government, 1 conceive, the legiſlature of the ſtate, by the ex-
preſſed or implied aſſent of the people, or the people of
the ſtate, under the direction of the government of it,
may accede to the federal compact : Nor do I conceive
it to be neceſſarily a part of a confederacy of ſtates, that
each have an equal voice in the general councils. A
confederated republic being organized, each ſtate muſt
retain powers for managing its internal police, and all
delegate to the union power to manage general concerns:
The quantity of power the union muſt poſſeſs is one
thing, the mode of exerciſing the powers given, is quite
a different conſideration and it is the mode of exerciſing them, that makes one of the eſſential diſtinctions between one entire or conſolidated government, and a federal republic ; that is, however the government may be
organized, if the laws of the union, in moſt important
concerns, as in levying and collecting taxes, raiſing
troops, &c. operate immediately upon the perſons and
property

property of individuals, and not on states, extend to organizing the militia, &c. the government, as to its administration, as to making and executing laws, is not federal, but consolidated To illustrate my idea—the union makes a requisition, and assigns to each state its quota of men or monies wanted; each state, by its own laws and officers, in its own way, furnishes its quota: here the state governments stand between the union and individuals ; the laws of the union operate only on states, as such, and federally : Here nothing can be done without the meetings of the state legislatures—but in the other case the union, though the state legislatures should not meet for years together, proceeds immediately, by its own laws and officers, to levy and collect monies of individuals, to inlist men, form armies, &c. here the laws of the union operate immediately on the body of the people, on persons and property ; in the same manner the laws of one entire consolidated government operate.— These two modes are very distinct, and in their operation and consequences have directly opposite tendencies: The first makes the existence of the state governments indispensable, and throws all the detail business of levying and collecting the taxes, &c. into the hands of those governments, and into the hands, of course, of many thousand officers solely created by, and dependent on the state. The last entirely excludes the agency of the respective states, and throws the whole business of levying and collecting taxes, &c. into the hands of many thousand officers solely created by, and dependent upon the union, and makes the existence of the state government of no consequence in the case. It is true, congress in raising any given sum in direct taxes, must by the constitution, raise so much of it in one state, and so much in another, by a fixed rule, which most of the states some time since agreed to : But this does not effect the principle in question, it only secures each state against any arbitrary proportions. The federal mode is perfectly safe and eligible, founded in the true spirit of a confederated republic ; there could be no possible exception to it. did we not find by experience, that the states will sometimes neglect to comply with the

the reasonable requisitions of the union. It being according to the fundamental principles of federal republics, to raise men and monies by requisitions, and for the states individually to organize and train the militia, I conceive. there can be no reason whatever for departing from them, except this, that the states sometimes neglect to comply with reasonable requisitions, and that it is dangerous to attempt to compel a delinquent state by force, as it may often produce a war. We ought, therefore, to enquire attentively, how extensive the evils to be guarded against are, and cautiously limit the remedies to the extent of the evils. I am not about to defend the confederation, or to charge the proposed constitution with imperfections not in it ; but we ought to examine facts, and strip them of the false colourings often given them by incautious observations. by unthinking or designing men. We ought to premise, that laws for raising men and monies, even in consolidated governments, are not often punctually complied with Historians, except in extraordinary cases, but very seldom take notice of the detail collection of taxes ; but these facts we have fully proved, and well attested ; that the most energetic governments have relinquished taxes frequently, which were of many years standing These facts amply prove, that taxes affessed, have remained many years uncollected. I agree there have been instances in the republics of Greece, Holland &c. in the course of several centuries, of states neglecting to pay their quotas of requisitions. but it is a circumstance certainly deserving of attention. whether these nations which have depended on requisitions principally for their defence, have not raised men and monies nearly as punctually as entire governments, which have taxed directly ; whether we have not found the latter as often distressed for the want of troops and monies as the former. It has been said that the Amphictionic council, and the Germanic head, have not possessed sufficient powers to controul the members of the republic in a proper manner. Is this, if true, to be imputed to requisitions ? Is it not principally to be imputed to the unequal powers of those members, connected with this important circumstance,

that

that each member poffeffed power to league itfelf with
foreign powers, and powerful neighbours, without the
confent of the head. After all, has not the Germanic
body a government as good as its neighbours in general ? and did not the Grecian republic remain united
feveral centuries, and form the theatre of human great-
nefs ? No government in Europe has commanded monies
more plentifully than the government of Holland. As
to the United States, the feparate ftates lay taxes directly, and the union calls for taxes by way of requifitions ;
and is it a fact, that more monies are due in proportion
on requifitions in the United States, than on the ftate
taxes directly laid ?—It is but about ten years fince
congrefs begun to make requifitions, and in that time,
the monies, &c. required, and the bounties given for
men required of the ftates, have amounted, fpecie value,
to about 36 millions dollars, about 24 millions of dollars of which have been actually paid ; and a very confiderable part of the 12 millions not paid, remains fo
not fo much from the neglect of the ftates, as from the
fudden changes in paper money, &c. which in a great
meafure rendered payments of no fervice, and which
often induced the union indirectly to relinquifh one demand, by making another in a different form. Before
we totally condemn requifitions, we ought to confider
what immenfe bounties the ftates gave, and what prodigious exertions they made in the war, in order to comply with the requifitions of congrefs ; and if fince the
peace they have been delinquent, ought we not carefully to enquire, whether that delinquency is to be imputed folely to the nature of requifitions ? ought it not
in part to be imputed to two other caufes ? I mean firft,
an opinion, that has extenfively prevailed, that the requifitions for domeftic intereft have not been founded on
juft principles ; and fecondly, the circumftance, that
the government itfelf, by propofing impofts, &c. has
departed virtually from the conftitutional fyftem ; which
propofed changes, like all changes propofed in government, produce an inattention and negligence in the execution of the government in being.

U   I

I am not for depending wholly on requisitions; but I mention these few facts to shew they are not so totally futile as many pretend. For the truth of many of these facts I appeal to the public records; and for the truth of the others, I appeal to many republican characters, who are best informed in the affairs of the United States. Since the peace, and till the convention reported, the wisest men in the United States generally supposed, that certain limited funds would answer the purposes of the union: and though the states are by no means in so good a condition as I wish they were, yet, I think, I may very safely affirm, they are in a better condition than they would be had congress always possessed the powers of taxation now contended for. The fact is admitted, that our federal government does not possess sufficient powers to give life and vigor to the political system; and that we experience disappointments, and several inconveniencies; but we ought carefully to distinguish those which are merely the consequences of a severe and tedious war, from those which arise from defects in the federal system. There has been an entire revolution in the United States within thirteen years, and the least we can compute the waste of labour and property at, during that period, by the war, is three hundred million of dollars. Our people are like a man just recovering from a severe fit of sickness. It was the war that disturbed the course of commerce, introduced floods of paper money, the stagnation of credit, and threw many valuable men out of steady business. From these sources our greatest evils arise; men of knowledge and reflection must perceive it;—but then, have we not done more in three or four years past, in repairing the injuries of the war, by repairing houses and estates, restoring industry, frugality, the fisheries, manufactures, &c. and thereby laying the foundation of good government, and of individual and political happiness, than any people ever did in a like time; we must judge from a view of the country and facts, and not from foreign newspapers, or our own, which are printed chiefly in the commercial towns, where imprudent living, imprudent importations, and many unexpected disappointments,

ments, have produced a defpondency, and a difpofition
to view every thing on the dark fide. Some of the evils
we feel, all will agree, ought to be imputed to the defective adminiftration of the governments. From thefe
and various confiderations, I am very clearly of opinion, that the evils we fuftain, merely on account of
the defects of the confederation, are but as a feather
in the balance againft a mountain, compared with thofe
which would, infallibly, be the refult of the lofs of
general liberty, and that happinefs men enjoy under a
frugal, free, and mild government.

Heretofore we do not feem to have feen danger any
where, but in giving power to congrefs, and now no
where but in congrefs wanting powers; and, without
examining the extent of the evils to be remedied, by one
ftep, we are for giving up to congrefs almoft all powers
of any importance without limitation. The defects of
the confederation are extravagantly magnified, and every
fpecies of pain we feel imputed to them: and hence it
is inferred, there muft be a total change of the principles, as well as forms of government: and in the main
point, touching the federal powers. we reft all on a logical
inference, totally inconfiftent with experience and found
political reafoning.

It is faid, that as the federal head muft make peace
and war, and provide for the common defence, it ought
to poffefs all powers neceffary to that end: that powers
unlimited, as to the purfe and fword, to raife men and
monies, and form the militia, are neceffary to that end;
and, therefore, the federal head ought to poffefs them.
This reafoning is far more fpecious than folid: it is neceffary that thefe powers fo exift in the body politic, as
to be called into exercife whenever neceffary for the
public fafety; but it is by no means true, that the man,
or congrefs of men, whofe duty it more immediately is
to provide for the common defence, ought to poffefs
them without limitation. But clear it is, that if fuch
men, or congrefs, be not in a fituation to hold them
without danger to liberty, he or they ought not to poffefs them. It has long been thought to be a well founded pofition, that the purfe and fword ought not to be
placed

placed in the fame hands in a free government. Our
wife anceſtors have carefully ſeparated them—placed the
ſword in the hands of their king, even under conſiderable limitations, and the purſe in the hands of the commons alone : yet the king makes peace and war, and it
is his duty to provide for the common defence of the
nation. This authority at leaſt goes thus far—that a
nation, well verſed in the ſcience of government, does
not conceive it to be neceſſary or expedient for the man
entruſted with the common defence and general tranquility, to poſſeſs unlimitedly the powers in queſtion,
or even in any conſiderable degree. Could he, whoſe
duty it is to defend the public, poſſeſs in himſelf independently, all the means of doing it conſiſtent with the
public good, it might be convenient : but the people of
England know that their liberties and happineſs would
be in infinitely greater danger from the king's unlimited
poſſeſſion of theſe powers, than from all external enemies and internal commotions to which they might be
expoſed : therefore, though they have made it his duty
to guard the empire, yet they have wiſely placed in
other hands, the hands of their repreſentatives, the
power to deal out and controul the means. In Holland
their high mightineſſes muſt provide for the common
defence, but for the means they depend, in a conſiderable degree, upon requiſitions made on the ſtate or local aſſemblies. Reaſon and facts evince that however
convenient it might be for an executive magiſtrate, or
federal head, more immediately charged with the national defence and ſafety, ſolely, directly, and independently to poſſeſs all the means ; yet ſuch magiſtrate,
or head, never ought to poſſeſs them, if thereby the
public liberties ſhall be endangered. The powers in
queſtion never have been, by nations wiſe and free, de-
poſited, nor can they ever be, with ſafety, any where,
but in the principal members of the national ſyſtem ;—
where theſe form one entire government, as in Great-
Britain, they are ſeparated and lodged in the principal
members of it. But in a federal republic, there is
quite a different organization : the people form this
kind of government, generally, becauſe their territories
are

are too extenfive to admit of their affembling in one
legiflature, or of executing the laws on free principles
under one entire government. They convene in their
local affemblies, for local purpofes, and for managing their
internal concerns, and unite their ftates under a federal
head for general purpofes. It is the effential charac-
teriftic of a confederated republic, that this head be dependant on, and kept withinlimited bounds by, the local
governments ; and it is becaufe, in thefe alone, in fact,
the people can be fubftantially affembled or reprefented.
It is, therefore, we very univerfally fee, in this kind of
government, the congreffional powers placed in a few
hands, and accordingly limited, and fpecifically enumerated : and the local affemblies ftrong and well guarded,
and compofed of numerous members. Wife men will
always place the controuling power where the people
are fubftantially collected by their reprefentatives. By
the propofed fyftem, the federal head will poffefs, without limitation, almoft every fpecies of power that can,
in its exercife, tend to change the government, or to
endanger liberty ; while in it, I think it has been fully
fhewn, the people will have but the fhadow of reprefentation, and but the fhadow of fecurity for their rights
and liberties. In a confederated republic the divifion
of reprefentation, &c. in its nature, requires a correfpon-
dent divifion and depofit of powers relative to taxes and
military concerns : and I think the plan offered ftands
quite alone, in confounding the principles of governments in themfelves totally diftinct. I wifh not to ex-
culpate the ftates for their improper neglects in not
paying their quotas of requifitions ; but, in applying
the remedy, we muft be governed by reafon and facts.
It will not be denied, that the people have a right to
change the government when the majority chufe it, if
not reftrained by fome exifting compact—that they have
a right to difplace their rulers, and confequently to determine when their meafures are reafonable or not—and
that they have a right, at any time, to put a ftop to
thofe meafures they may deem prejudicial to them, by
fuch forms and negatives as they may fee fit to provide.
From all thefe, and many other well founded confider-

X   ation

ations, I need not mention, a queſtion ariſes, what powers ſhall there be delegated to the federal head, to inſure ſafety, as well as energy, in the government ? I think there is a ſafe and proper medium pointed out by experience, by reaſon, and facts. When we have organized the government, we ought to give power to the union, ſo far only as experience and preſent circumſtances ſhall direct, with a reaſonable regard to time to come. Should future circumſtances, contrary to our expectations, require that further powers be transferred to the union, we can do it far more eaſily. than get back thoſe we may now imprudently give. The ſyſtem propoſed is untried : candid advocates and oppoſers admit, that it is, in a degree, a mere experiment, and that its organization is weak and imperfect ; ſurely then, the ſafe ground is cautiouſly to veſt power in it, and when we are ſure we have given enough for ordinary exigencies, to be extremely careful how we delegate powers, which, in common caſes, muſt neceſſarily be uſeleſs or abuſed, and of very uncertain effect in uncommon ones.

By giving the union power to regulate commerce, and to levy and collect taxes by impoſts, we give it an extenſive authority, and permanent productive funds, I believe quite as adequate to the preſent demands of the union, as exiſes and direct taxes can be made to the preſent demands of the ſeparate ſtates. The ſtate governments are now about four times as expenſive as that of the union ; and their ſeveral ſtate debts added together, are nearly as large as that of the union—Our impoſt duties ſince the peace have been almoſt as productive as the other ſources of taxation, and when under one general ſyſtem of regulations, the probability is, that thoſe duties will be very conſiderably increaſed : Indeed the repreſentation propoſed will hardly juſtify giving to congreſs unlimited powers to raiſe taxes by impoſts, in addition to the other powers the union muſt neceſſarily have. It is ſaid, that if congreſs poſſeſs only authority to raiſe taxes by impoſts, trade probably will be overburdened with taxes, and the taxes of the union be found inadequate to any uncommon exigencies : To this we may obſerve, that trade generally finds its own level,

and

and will naturally and neceffarily heave off any undue
burdens laid upon it : further, if congrefs alone poffefs
the impoft, and alfo unlimited power to raife monies by
excifes and direct taxes, there muft be much more danger that two taxing powers, the union and ftates, will
carry excifes and direct taxes to an unreafonable extent,
efpecially as thefe have not the natural boundaries taxes
on trade have. However, it is not my object to propofe
to exclude congrefs from raifing monies by internal taxes,
as by duties, excifes, and direct taxes but my opinion
is, that congrefs, efpecially in its propofed organization, ought not to raife monies by internal taxes. except
in ftrict conformity to the federal plan ; that is, by the
agency of the ftate governments in all cafes, except
where a ftate fhall neglect, for an unreafonable time, to
pay its quota of a requifition ; and never where fo many
of the ftate legiflatures as reprefent a majority of the
people, fhall formally determine an excife law or requifition is improper, in their next feffion after the fame be
laid before them. We ought always to recollect that
the evil to be guarded againft is found by our own experience, and the experience of others, to be mere neglect in the ftates to pay their quotas ; and power in the
union to levy and collect the neglecting ftates' qnotas
with intereft, is fully adequate to the evil. By this federal plan, with this exception mentioned, we fecure
the means of collecting the taxes by the ufual procefs of
law, and avoid the evil of attempting to compel or coerce
a ftate and we avoid alfo a circumftance, which never
yet could be, and I am fully confident never can be, admitted in a free federal republic ; I mean a permanent
and continued fyftem of tax laws of the union, executed
in the bowels of the ftates by many thoufand officers,
dependent as to the affeffing and collecting federal taxes,
folely upon the union. On every principle then, we
ought to provide, that the union render an exact account
of all monies raifed by impofts and other taxes ; and that
whenever monies fhall be wanted for the purpofes of the
union, beyond the proceeds of the impoft duties, requifitions fhall be made on the ftates for the monies fo
wanted ; and that the power of laying and collecting

fhall

fhall never be exercifed, except in cafes where a ftate fhall neglect, a given time, to pay its quota. This mode feems to be ftrongly pointed out by the reafon of the cafe, and fpirit of the government; and I believe, there is 'no inftance to be found in a federal republic, where the congreffional powers ever extended generally to collecting monies by direct taxes or excifes. Creating all thefe reftrictions, ftill the powers of the union in matters of taxation, will be too unlimited; further checks, in my mind, are indifpenfably neceffary. Nor do I conceive, that as full a reprefentation as is practicable in the federal government, will afford fufficient fecurity: the ftrength of the government, and the confidence of the people, muft be collected principally in the local affemblies; every part or branch of the federal head muft be feeble, and unfafely trufted with large powers. A government poffeffed of more power than its conftituent parts will juftify, will not only probably abufe it, but be unequal to bear its own burden; it may as foon be deftroyed by the preffure of power, as languifh and perifh for want of it.

There are two ways further of raifing checks, and guarding againft undue combinations and influence in a federal fyftem. The firft is, in levying taxes, raifing and keeping up armies, in building navies, in forming plans for the militia, and in appropriating monies for the fupport of the military, to require the attendance of a large proportion of the federal reprefentatives, as two thirds or three-fourths of them; and in paffing laws, in thefe important cafes, to require the confent of two-thirds or three-fourths of the members prefent. The fecond is, by requiring that certain important laws of the federal head, as a requifition or a law for raifing monies by excife fhall be laid before the ftate legiflatures, and if difapproved of by a given number of them, fay by as many of them as reprefent a majority of the people, the law fhall have no effect. Whether it would be advifeable to adopt both, or either of thefe checks, I will not undertake to determine. We have feen them both exift in confederated republics. The firft exifts fubftantially in the confederation, and will exift

exift in fome meafure in the plan propofed, as in chufing a prefident by the houfe, in expelling members ; in the fenate, in making treaties, and in deciding on impeach-ments, and in the whole in altering the conftitution. The laft exifts in the United Netherlands, but in a much greater extent. The firft is founded on this prin-ciple, that thefe important meafures may, fometimes, be adopted by a bare quorum of members, perhaps, from a few ftates, and that a bare majority of the fede-ral reprefentatives may frequently be of the ariftocracy, or fome particular interefts, connections, or parties in the community, and governed by motives, views, and inclinations not compatible with the general intereft.—The laft is founded on this principle, that the people will be fubftantially reprefented, only in their ftate or local affemblies ; that their principal fecurity muft be found in them ; and that, therefore, they ought to have ultimately a conftitutional controul over fuch interefting meafures.

I have often heard it obferved, that our people are well informed, and will not fubmit to oppreffive go-vernments ; that the ftate governments will be their ready advocates, and poffefs their confidence, mix with them, and enter into all their wants and feelings. This is all true ; but of what avail will thefe circumftances be, if the ftate governments, thus allowed to be the guar-dians of the people, poffefs no kind of power by the forms of the focial compact, to ftop in their paffage, the laws of congrefs injurious to the people. State go-vernments muft ftand and fee the law take place ; they may complain and petition— fo may individuals ; the members of them, in extreme cafes, may refift, on the principles of felf-defence—fo may the people and in-dividuals.

It has been obferved, that the people, in extenfive territories, have more power, compared with that of their rulers, than in fmall ftates. Is not directly the oppofite true ? The people in a fmall ftate can unite and act in concert, and with vigour ; but in large ter-ritories, the men who govern find it more eafy to unite, while people cannot ; while they cannot collect the opi-

nions

nions of each part, while they move to different points, and one part is often played off againſt the other.

It has been aſſerted, that the confederate head of a republic at beſt, is in general weak and dependent ; — that the people will attach themſelves to, and ſupport their local governments, in all diſputes with the union. Admit the fact : is it any way to remove the inconvenience by accumulating powers upon a weak organization ? The fact is, that the detail adminiſtration of affairs, in this mixed republics, depends principally on the local governments ; and the people would be wretched without them : and a great proportion of ſocial happineſs depends on the internal adminiſtration of juſtice, and on internal police. The ſplendor of the monarch, and the power of the government are one thing. The happineſs of the ſubject depends on very different cauſes : but it is to the latter, that the beſt men, the greateſt ornaments of human nature, have moſt carefully attended : it is to the former tyrants and oppreſſors have always aimed,

The FEDERAL FARMER.

L E T T E R   XVIII.

JANUARY 25, 1788.

DEAR SIR,

I AM perſuaded, a federal head never was formed, that poſſeſſed half the powers which it could carry into full effect, altogether independently of the ſtate or local governments, as the one, the convention has propoſed, will poſſeſs. Should the ſtate legiſlatures never meet, except merely for chuſing federal ſenators and appointing electors, once in four and ſix years, the federal head may go on for ages to make all laws relative to the following ſubjects, and by its own courts, officers, and proviſions, carry them into full effect, and to any extent it may deem for the general welfare ; that

is,

is, for *raiſing taxes*, borrowing and coining monies, and
for applying them—for forming and governing *armies*
and *navies* and for directing their operations—for regulating commerce with foreign nations, and among
the ſeveral ſtates, and with the Indian tribes—for regulating *bankruptcies*, weights and meaſures, poſt-offices
and poſt-roads, and captures on land and water—for
eſtabliſhing a uniform rule of naturalization, and for
promoting the progreſs of ſcience and uſeful arts—for
defining and puniſhing piracies and felonies committed
on the high ſeas, the offences of counterfeiting the
ſecurities and current coin of the United States, and
offences againſt the law of nations, and for regulating
all maritime concerns—for *organizing*, *arming* and *diſ-
ciplining* the militia (the reſpective ſtates training them,
and appointing the officers)—for *calling them forth*
when wanted, and for governing them when in the ſervice of the union—for the *ſole and excluſive government*
of a federal city or town, not exceeding ten miles
ſquare, and of places ceded for forts, magazines arſe-
nals, dock-yards, and other needful buildings—for
granting letters of marque and repriſal, and making
war—for regulating the *times, places*, and *manner of
holding elections* for ſenators and repreſentatives—for
making and concluding all treaties, and carrying them
into execution—for judicially deciding all queſtions ariſing on the conſtitution laws, and treaties of the union,
in law and equity, and queſtions ariſing on ſtate laws
alſo, where ambaſſadors, other public miniſters, and
conſuls where the United States, individual ſtates, or
a ſtate, where *citizens of different ſtates*, and where foreign
ſtates, or a *foreign ſubject*, are parties or party—for impeaching and trying federal officers—for deciding on
elections, and for expelling members, &c. All theſe
enumerated powers we muſt examine and contemplate
in all their extent and various branches, and then reflect,
that the federal head will have full power to make all
laws whatever reſpecting them; and for carrying into
full effect all powers veſted in the union, in any department, or officers of it, by the conſtitution, in order to
ſee the full extent of the federal powers, which will be
ſupreme,

supreme, and exercised by that head at pleasure, con
fo ming to the few limitations mentioned in the constitution Indeed, I conceive, it is impossible to see them
in their full extent at present : we see vast undefined
powers lodged in a weak organization, but cannot, by
the enquiries of months and years, clearly discern them
in all their numerous branches. These powers in feeble
hands, must be tempting objects for ambition and a love
of power and fame.

But, say the advocates, they are all necessary for forming an energetic federal government ; all necessary in
the hands of the union, for the common defence and
general welfare. In these great points they appear to
me to go from the end to the means, and from the means
to the end, perpetually begging the question I think
in the course of these letters, I shall sufficiently prove,
that some of these powers need not be lodged in the
hands of the union—that others ought to be exercised
under better checks, and in part, by the agency of the
states—some I have already considered, some in my
mind, are not liable to objections. and the others, I
shall briefly notice in this closing letter.

The power to controul the military forces of the
country, as well as the revenues of it, requires serious
attention. Here again I must premise, that a federal
republic is a compound system, made up of constituent
parts. each essential to the whole : we must then expect
the real friends of such a system will always be very anxious for the security and preservation of each part. and
to this end, that each constitutionally possesses its natural portion of power and influence —and that it will
constantly be an object of concern to them, to see one
part armed at all points by the constitution, and in a
manner destructive in the end, even of its own existence,
and the others left constitutionally defenceless.

The military forces of a free country may be considered under three general descriptions 1. The militia.
2. the navy—and the regular troops and the whole
ought ever to be, and understood to be. in strict subordination to the civil authority. and that regular troops,
and select corps, ought not to be kept up without evident

dent neceſſity. Stipulations in the conſtitution to this
effect, are perhaps, too general to be of much ſervice,
except merely to impreſs on the minds of the people
and ſoldiery, that the military ought ever to be ſubject to the civil authority, &c. But particular attention, and many more definite ſtipulations, are highly
neceſſary to render the military ſafe, and yet uſeful in
a free government ; and in a federal republic, where
the people meet in diſtinct aſſemblies, many ſtipulations are neceſſary to keep a part from tranſgreſſing,
which would be unneceſſary checks againſt the whole
met in one legiſlature, in one entire government.—
A militia, when properly formed, are in fact the
people themſelves, and render regular troops in a great
meaſure unneceſſary. The powers to form and arm the
militia, to appoint their officers, and to command their
ſervices, are very important ; nor ought they in a confederated republic to be lodged, ſolely, in any one
member of the government. Firſt, the conſtitution
ought to ſecure a genuine and guard againſt a ſelect
militia, by providing that the militia ſhall always be
kept well organized, armed, and diſciplined, and include, according to the paſt and general uſuage of the
ſtates, all men capable of bearing arms ; and that all
regulations tending to render this general militia uſeleſs
and defenceleſs, by eſtabliſhing ſelect corps of militia,
or diſtinct bodies of military men, not having permanent intereſts and attachments in the community to be
avoided. I am perſuaded, I need not multiply words
to convince you of the value and ſolidity of this principle, as it reſpects general liberty, and the duration of a
free and mild government : having this principle well fixed
by the conſtitution, then the federal head may preſcribe
a general uniform plan, on which the reſpective ſtates
ſhall form and train the militia, appoint their officers, and
ſolely manage them, except when called into the ſervice
of the union, and when called into that ſervice, they
may be commanded and governed by the union. This
arrangement combines energy and ſafety in it ; it places
the ſword in the hands of the ſolid intereſt of the community, and not in the hands of men deſtitute of pro-

Y   perty,

perty, of principle, or of attachment to the fociety and government, who often form the felect corps of peace or ordinary eftablifhments : by it, the militia are the people, immediately under the management of the ftate governments, but on a uniform federal plan, and called into the fervice, command, and government of the union, when neceffary for the common defence and general tranquility. But, fay gentlemen, the general militia are for the moft part employed at home in their private concerns, cannot well be called out, or be depended upon ; that we muft have a felect militia ; that is, as I underftand it, particular corps or bodies of young men, and of men who have but little to do at home, particularly armed and difciplined in fome meafure, at the public expence, and always ready to take the field. Thefe corps, not much unlike regular troops, will ever produce an inattention to the general militia ; and the confequence has ever been, and always muft be, that the fubftantial men, having families and property, will generally be without arms, without knowing the ufe of them, and defencelefs ; whereas, to preferve liberty, it is effential that the whole body of the people always poffefs arms, and be taught alike, efpecially when young, how to ufe them ; nor does it follow from this, that all promifououfly muft go into actual fervice on every occafion. The mind that aims at a felect militia, muft be influenced by a truly anti republican principle ; and when we fee many men difpofed to practice upon it, whenever they can prevail, no wonder true republicans are for carefully guarding againft it. As a farther check, it may be proper to add, that the militia of any ftate fhall not remain in the fervice of the union, beyond a given period, without the exprefs confent of the ftate legiflature.

As to the navy, 1 do not fee that it can have any connection with the local governments. The want of employment for it, and the want of monies in the hands of the union, muft be its proper limitation. The laws for building or increafing it, as all the important laws mentioned in a former letter, touching military and money matters, may be checked by requiring the attendance

tendance of a large proportion of the reprefentatives, and the confent of a large proportion of thofe prefent, to pafs them as before mentioned.

By art. 1. fect. 8. "Congrefs fhall have *power to pro-*vide for organizing, arming, and difciplining the milit ia : *power to provide for*—does this imply any more than power to prefcribe a general uniform plan? And muft not the refpective ftates pafs laws (but in conformity to the plan) for forming and training the militia.

In the prefent ftate of mankind, and of conducting war, the government of every nation muft have power to raife and keep up regular troops: the queftion is, how fhall this power be lodged? In an entire government, as in Great-Britain, where the people affemble by their reprefentatives in one legiflature, there is no difficulty, it is of courfe properly lodged in that legiflature: But in a confederated republic, where the organization confifts of a federal head, and local governments, there is no one part in which it can be folely, and fafely lodged. By art. 1. fect. 8. "congrefs fhall have power to raife and fupport armies," &c. By art. 1. fect. 10. "no ftate, without the confent of congrefs, fhall keep troops, or fhips of war, in time of peace." It feems fit the union fhould direct the raifing of troops, and the union may do it in two ways; by requifitions on the ftates, or by direct taxes—the firft is moft conformable to the federal plan, and fafeft; and it may be improved, by giving the union power, by its own laws and officers, to raife the ftates quota that may neglect, and to charge it with the expence; and by giving a fixed quorum of the ftate legiflatures power to difapprove the requifition. There would be lefs danger in this power to raife troops, could the ftate governments keep a proper controul over the purfe and over the militia; but after all the precautions we can take, without evidently fettering the union too much, we muft give a large accumulation of powers to it, in thefe and other refpects. There is one check, which, I think, may be added with great propriety—that is, no land forces fhall be kept up, but by legiflative acts annually paffed by congrefs, and no appropriation of monies for

their

their fupport fhall be for a longer term than one year. This is the conftitutional practice in Great-Britain, and the reafons for fuch checks in the United States appear to be much ftronger. We may alfo require that thefe acts be paffed by a fpecial majority, as before mentioned. There is another mode ftill more guarded, and which feems to be founded in the true fpirit of a federal fyftem : it feems proper to divide thofe powers we can with fafety, lodge them in no one member of the government alone ; yet fubftantially to preferve their ufe, and to enfure duration to the government, by modifying the exercife of them—it is to empower congrefs to raife troops by direct levies, not exceeding a given number, fay 2000 in time of peace, and 12,000 in a time of war, and for fuch further troops as may be wanted, to raife them by requifitions qualified as before mentioned. By the above recited claufe no ftate fhall keep troops, &c. in time of peace—this clearly implies, it may do it in time of war : this muft be on the principle, that the union cannot defend all parts of the republic, and fuggefts an idea very repugnant to the general tendency of the fyftem propofed, which is to difarm the ftate governments : a ftate in a long war may collect forces fufficient to take the field againft the neighbouring ftates. This claufe was copied from the confederation, in which it was of more importance than in the plan propofed, becaufe under this the feparate ftates, probably, will have but fmall revenues.

By article 1. fection 8. congrefs fhall have power to eftablifh uniform laws on the fubject of bankruptcies, throughout the United States. It is to be obferved, that the feparate ftates have ever been in poffeffion of the power, and in the ufe of it, of making bankrupt laws, militia laws, and laws in fome other cafes, refpecting which, the new conftitution, when adopted, will give the union power to legiflate, &c.—but no words are ufed by the conftitution to exclude the jurifdiction of the feveral ftates, and whether they will be excluded or not, or whether they and the union will have concurrent jurifdiction or not, muft be determined by inference ; and from the nature of the fubject ; if the
power,

power, for inftance, to make uniform laws on the fubject of bankruptcies, is in its nature indivifible, or in
capable of being exercifed by two legiflatures independently, or by one in aid of the other, then the ftates
are excluded, and cannot legiflate at all on the fubject,
even though the union fhould neglect or find it impracticable to eftablifh uniform bankrupt laws. How far the
union will find it practicable to do this, time only can
fully determine. When we confider the extent of the
country, and the very different ideas of the different
parts in it, refpecting credit, and the mode of making
men's property liable for paying their debts, we may, I
think, with fome degree of certainty, conclude that the
union never will be able to eftablifh fuch laws; but if
practicable, it does not appear to me, on further reflection, that the union ought to have the power ; it does
not appear to me to be a power properly incidental to
a federal head, and, I believe, no one ever poffeffed it ;
it is a power that will immediately and extenfively interfere with the internal police of the feparate ftates, efpecially with their adminiftering juftic among their own
citizens. By giving this power to the union, we greatly extend the jurifdiction of the federal judiciary, as all
queftions arifing on bankrupt laws, being laws of the
union, even between citizens of the fame ftate, may be
tried in the federal courts ; and I think it may be
fhewn, that by the help of thefe laws, actions between
citizens of different ftates, and the laws of the federal
city, aided by no overftrained judicial fictions, almoft
all civil caufes may be drawn into thofe courts. We
muft be fenfible how cautious we ought to be in extend-
ing unneceffarily the jurifdiction of thofe courts, for
reafons I need not repeat. This article of power too,
will confiderably increafe, in the hands of the union, an
accumulation of powers, fome of a federal and fome of
a unfederal nature, too large without it.

The conftitution provides, that congrefs fhall have the
fole and exclufive government of what is called the fe-
federal city, a place not exceeding ten miles fquare, and
of all places ceded for forts, dock-yards, &c. I believe
this is a new kind of provifion in a federal republic ;

Z   it

it is repugnant to the fpirit of fuch a government, and
muft be founded in an apprehenfion of a hoftile difpofition between the federal head and the ftate governments ; and it is not improbable, that the fudden retreat
of congrefs from Philadelphia, firft gave rife to it.—
With this apprehenfion, we provide, the government
of the union fhall have fecluded places, cities, and
caftles of defence, which no ftate laws whatever fhall
invade. When we attentively examine this provifion in
all its confequences, it opens to view fcenes almoft
without bounds. A federal, or rather a national city,
ten miles fquare, containing a hundred fquare miles, is
about four times as large as London ; and for forts,
magazines, arfenals, dock-yards, and other needful buildings, congrefs may poffefs a number of places or towns
in each ftate. It is true, congrefs cannot have them unlefs the ftate legiflatures cede them ; but when once
ceded, they never can be recovered, and though the
general temper of the legiflatures may be averfe to fuch
ceffions, yet many opportunities and advantages may be
taken of particular times and circumftances of com-
plying affemblies, and of particular parties, to obtain
them. It is not improbable, that fome confiderable
towns or places, in fome intemperate moments, or influenced by tanti-republican principles, will petition to be ceded for the purpofes mentioned in the provifion. There are men, and even towns, in the beft
republics, which are often fond of withdrawing from
the government of them, whenever occafion fhall prefent. The cafe is ftill ftronger ; if the provifion in
queftion holds out allurements to attempt to withdraw,
the people of a ftate muft ever be fubject to ftate as
well as federal taxes ; but the federal city and places
will be fubject only to the latter, and to them by no
fixed proportion , nor of the taxes raifed in them, can
the feparate ftates demand any account of congrefs.—
Thefe doors opened for withdrawing from the ftate governments entirely, may, on other accounts, be very
alluring and pleafing to thofe anti-republican men who
prefer a place under the wings of courts.

If a federal town be neceffary for the refidence of
congrefs

congrefs and the public officers, it ought to be a fmall one, and the government of it fixed on republican and common law principles, carefully enumerated and eftablifhed by the conftitution. It is true, the ftates, when they fhall cede places, may ftipulate, that the laws and government of congrefs in them, fhall always be formed on fuch principles; but it is eafy to difcern, that the ftipulations of a ftate, or of the inhabitants of the place ceded, can be of but little avail againft the power and gradual encroachments of the union. The principles ought to be eftablifhed by the federal conftitution, to which all the ftates are parties; but in no event can there be any need of fo large a city and places for forts, &c. totally exempted from the laws and jurifdictions of the ftate governments. If I underftand the conftitution, the laws of congrefs, conftitutionally made, will have complete and fupreme jurifdiction to all federal pnrpofes, on every inch of ground in the United States, and exclufive jurifdiction on the high feas, and this by the higheft anthority, the confent of the people. Suppofe ten acres at Weft-Point fhall be ufed as a fort of the union, or a fea port town as a dock-yard, the laws of the union in thofe places refpecting the navy, forces of the union, and all federal objects, muft prevail, be noticed by all judges and officers, and executed accordingly: and I can difcern no one reafon for excluding from thefe places, the operation of ftate laws, as to mere ftate purpofes; for inftance, for the collection of ftate taxes in them, recovering debts, deciding queftions of property arifing within them on ftate laws, punifhing, by ftate laws, theft, trefpaffes, and offences eommitted in them by mere citizens againft the ftate laws.

The city. and all the places in which the union fhall have this exclufive jurifdiction, will be immediately under one entire government, that of the federal head; and be no part of any ftate, and confequently no part of the United States. The inhabitants of the federal city and places, will be as much exempt from the laws and controul of the ftate governments, as the people of Canada or Nova Scotia will be. Neither the laws of the

Z 2   ftates

ftates refpecting taxes, the militia, crimes or property, will extend to them ; nor is there a fingle ftipulation in the conftitution, that the inhabitants of this city, and thefe places, fhall be governed by laws founded on principles of freedom. All queftions, civil and criminal, arifing on the laws of thefe places, which muft be the laws of congrefs, muft be decided in the federal courts; and alfo, all queftions that may, by fuch judicial fictions as thefe courts may confider reafonable, be fuppofed to arife within this city, or any of thefe places, may be brought into thefe courts ; and by a very common legal fiction, any perfonal contract may be fuppofed to have been made in any place. A contract made in Georgia may be fuppofed to have been made in the federal city, in Pennfylvania; the courts will admit the fiction, and not in thefe cafes, make it a ferious queftion, where it was in fact made. Every fuit in which an inhabitant of a federal diftrict may be a party, of courfe may be inftituted in the federal courts—alfo, every fuit in which it may be alledged, and not denied, that a party in it is an inhabitant of fuch a diftrict—alfo, every fuit to which a foreign ftate or fubject, the union, a ftate, citizens of different ftates, in fact, or by reafonable legal fictions, may be a party or parties : And thus, by means of bankrupt laws, federal diftricts, &c. almoft all judicial bufinefs, I apprehend, may be carried into the federal courts, without effentially departing from the ufual courfe of judicial proceedings. The courts in Great Britain have acquired their powers, and extended, very greatly, their jurifdictions by fuch fictions and fuppofitions as I have mentioned. The conftitution, in thefe points, certainly involves in it principles, and almoft hidden cafes, which may unfold, and in time exhibit confequences we hardly think of. The power of naturalization, when viewed in connection with the judicial powers and cafes, is, in my mind, of very doubtful extent. By the conftitution itfelf, the citizens of each ftate will be naturalized citizens of every ftate, to the general purpofes of inftituting fuits, claiming the benefits of the laws, &c. And in order to give the federal courts jurifdiction of an action, between citizens of the fame ftate,

in common acceptation, may not a court allow the plain-
tiff to fay, he is a citizen of one ftate, and the defend-
ant a citizen of another, without carrying legal fictions,
fo far, by any means, as they have been carried by the
courts of King's Bench and Exchequer, in order to
bring caufes within their cognizance—Further, the federal city and diftricts, will be totally diftinct from any
ftate, and a citizen of a ftate will not of courfe be a
fubject of any of them ; and to avail himfelf of the privileges and immunities of them, mnft he not be naturalized by congrefs in them ? and may not congrefs make
any proportion of the citizens of the ftates naturalized
fubjects of the federal city and diftricts, and thereby en-
title them to fue or defend, in all cafes, in the federal
courts ? I have my doubts, and many fenfible men I
find, have their doubts, on thefe points ; and we ought
to obferve, they muft be fettled in the courts of law, by
their rules, diftinctions, and fictions. To avoid many
of thefe intricacies and difficulties, and to avoid the undue and unneceffary extenfion of the federal judicial
powers, it appears to me that no federal diftricts ought
to be allowed, and no federal city or town, except perhaps a fmall town, in which the government fhall be
republican, but in which congrefs fhall have no jurifdiction over the inhabitants, but in common with the
other inhabitants of the ftates. Can the union want, in
fuch a town, any thing more than a right to the foil on
which it may fet its buildings, and extenfive jurifdiction
over the federal buildings, and property, its own members, officers, and fervants in it ? As to all federal objects, the union will have complete jurifdiction over
them, of courfe any where, and every where. I ftill
think, that no actions ought to be allowed to be brought
in the federal courts, between citizens of different ftates,
at leaft, unlefs the caufe be of very confiderable importance : that no action againft a ftate government, by any
citizen or foreigner, ought to be allowed ; and no action, in which a foreign fubject is party, at leaft, unlefs
it be of very confiderable importance, ought to be inftituted in the federal courts—I confefs, I can fee no reafon whatever, for a foreigner, or for citizens of different

ent ſtates, carrying ſixpenny cauſes into the federal
courts; I think the ſtate courts will be found by experience, to be bottomed on better principles, and to ad-
miniſter juſtice better than the federal courts.

The difficulties and dangers I have ſuppóſed, will
reſult from ſo large a federal city, and federal diſtricts,
from the extenſion of the federal judicial powers, &c.
are not, I conceive, merely poſſible, but probable I
think, pernicious political conſeqúences will follow from
them, and from the federal city eſpecially, for very obvious reaſons, a few of which I will mention.

We muſt obſerve, that the citizens of a ſtate will be
ſubject to ſtate as well as federal taxes, and the inhabitants of the federal city and diſtricts, only to ſuch
taxes as congreſs may lay—We are not to ſuppoſe all
our people are attached to free government, and the
principles of the common law but that many thouſands
of them will prefer a city governed, not on republican
principles—This city, and the government of it, muſt
indubitably take their tone from the characters of the
men, who from the nature of its ſituation and inſtituti-
on, muſt collect there. This city will not be eſtabliſhed
for productive labour, for mercantile, or mechanic induſtry ; but for the reſidence of government, its officers
and attendants. If hereafter it ſhould ever become a
place of trade and induſtry, in the early periods of its
exiſtence, when its laws and government muſt receive
their fixed tone, it muſt be a mere court, with its appendages, the executive, congreſs, the law courts, gentlemen of fortune and pleaſure, with all the officers, attendants, ſuitors, expectants and dependants on the
whole, however brilliant and honourable this collection may be, if we expect it will have any ſincere attachments to ſimple and frugal republicaniſn, to that liberty and mild government, which is dear to the laborious
part of a free people, we moſt aſſuredly deceive ourſelves.
This early collection will draw to it men from all parts
of the country, of a like political deſcription : we ſee
them looking towards the place already.

Such a city, or town, containing a hundred ſquare
miles, muſt ſoon be the great, the viſible, and dazzling
centre,

centre, the miftrefs of fafhions, and the fountain of politics. There may be a free or fhackled prefs in this
city, and the ftreams which may iffue from it may over-
flow the country, and they will be poifonous or pure,
as the fountain may be corrupt or not. But not to
dwell on a fubject that muft give pain to the virtuous
friends of freedom, I will only add, can a free and
enlightened people create a common head fo extenfive,
fo prone to corruption and flavery, as this city probably
will be, when they have it in their power to form one
pure and chafte, frugal and republican.

Under the confederation congrefs has no power
whereby to govern its own officers and fervant ; a federal town, in which congrefs might have fpecial jurifdiction, might be expedient ; but under the new conftitution, without a federal town, congrefs will have all
neceffary powers of courfe over its officers and fervants ;
indeed it will have a complete fyftem of powers to all
the federal purpofes mentioned in the conftitution ; fo
that the reafon for a federal town under the confederation, will by no means exift under the conftitution.—
Even if a trial by jury fhould be admitted in the federal
city, what man, with any ftate attachments or republican virtue about him, will fubmit to be tried by a
jury of it.

I might obferve more particularly upon feveral other
parts of the conftitution propofed ; but it has been uniformly my object in examining a fubject fo extenfive,
and difficult in many parts to be illuftrated, to avoid
unimportant things, and not to dwell upon points not
very material. The rule for apportioning requifitions
on the ftates, having fome time fince been agreed to by
eleven ftates, I have viewed as fettled. The ftipulation
that congrefs, after twenty one years may prohibit the
importation of flaves, is a point gained, if not fo favourable as could be wifhed for. As monopolies in trade perhaps, can in no cafe be ufeful, it might not be amifs to provide exprefsly againft them. I wifh the power to reprive
and pardon was more cautioufly lodged, and under fome
limitations. I do not fee why congrefs fhould be allowed

lowed to confent that a perfon may accept a prefent, office, or title of a foreign prince, &c. As to the ftate governments, as well as the federal, are effential parts of the fyftem, why fhould not the oath taken by the officers be exprefsly to fupport the whole? As to debts due to and from the union, I think the conftitution intends, on examining art. 4. fect. 8. and art. 6. that they fhall ftand on the fame ground under the conftituti-on as under the confederation. In the article refpecting amendments, it is ftipulated, that no ftate fhall ever be de-prived of its equal vote in the fenate without its confent ; and that alterations may be made by the confent of three-fourths of the ftates. Stipulations to bind the majority of the people may ferve one purpofe, to prevent frequent motions for change ; but thefe attempts to bind the majority, generally give occafion for breach of contract. The ftates all agreed about feven years ago, that the confederation fhould remain unaltered, unlefs every ftate fhould agree to alterations : but we now fee it agreed by the convention, and four ftates, that the old confederacy fhall be deftroyed, and a new one, of nine ftates, be erected, if nine only fhall come in. Had we agreed, that a majority fhould alter the confederation, a majority's agreeing would have bound the reft : but now we muft break the old league, unlefs all the ftates agree to alter, or not proceed with adopting the confti-tution. Whether the adoption by nine ftates will not produce a nearly equal and dangerous divifion of the people for and aginft the conftitution—whether the circumftances of the country were fuch as to juftify the hazarding a probability of fuch a fituation, I fhall not undertake to determine. I fhall leave it to be deter-mine hereafter, whether nine ftates, under a new federal compact, can claim the benefits of any treaties made with a confederation of thirteen, under a diftinct com-pact and form of exiftence—whether the new confede-racy can recover debts due to the old confederacy, or the arrears of taxes due from the ftates excluded.

It has been well obferved, that our country is exten-five, and has no external enemies to prefs the parts together,

together : that, therefore, their union muſt depend on
ſtrong internal ties. I differ with the gentlemen who
make theſe obervations only in this, they hold the ties
ought to be ſtrengthened by a conſiderable degree of
internal conſolidation. and my object is to form them
and ſtrengthen them, on pure federal principles. Whatever may be the fate of many valuable and neceſſary
amendments in the conſtitution propoſed, the ample
diſcuſſion and reſpectable oppoſition it will receive, will
have a good effect— they will operate to produce a mild
and prudent adminiſtration, and to put the wheels of
the whole ſyſtem in motion on proper principles—they
will evince, that true republican principles and attachments are ſtill alive and formidable in this country.
Theſe, in view. I believe, even men quite diſpoſed to
make a bad uſe of the ſyſtem, will long heſitate before
they will reſolve to do it._ A majority, from a view of
our ſituation. and influenced by many conſiderations,
may acquieſe in the adoption of this conſtitution ; but,
it is evident that a very g eat majority of the people of
the United States. think it, in many parts, an unneceſſary and unadviſeaole departure from true republican
and federal principles.

THE FEDERAL FARMER.

To the Republican.

OBSERVATIONS

On the new CONSTITUTION, *and on the* Federal
and State CONVENTIONS.

By a COLUMBIAN PATRIOT.

Sic transit gloria Americana.

MANKIND may amuse themselves with theoretick systems
of liberty, and trace its social and moral effects on sci-
ences, virtue, industry, and every improvement of which the
human mind is capable ; but we can only discern its true value by the practical and wretched effects of slavery ; and thus
dreadfully will they be realized, when the inhabitants of the
Eastern States are dragging out a miserable existence, *only* on
the gleanings of their fields ; and the Southern, blessed with a
softer and more fertile climate, are languishing in hopeless poverty ; and when asked, what is become of the flower of their
crop, and the rich produce of their farms—they may answer in
the hapless stile of the Man of *La Mancha*,—" The steward of
" my Lord has seized and sent it to *Madrid*."——Or, in the
more literal language of truth, The *exigencies* of government
require that the collectors of the revenue should transmit it to
the *Federal City*.
　Animated with the firmest zeal for the interest of this country, the peace and union of the American States, and the freedom and happiness of a people who have made the most costly
sacrifices in the cause of liberty,—who have braved the power
of Britain, weathered the convulsions of war, and waded thro'
the blood of friends and foes to establish their independence and
to support the freedom of the human mind ; I cannot silently
witness

witnefs this degradation without calling on them, before they are compelled to blufh at their own fervitude, and to turn back their languid eyes on their loft liberties—to confider, that the charafter of nations generally changes at the moment of revolution.——Aud when patriotifm is difcountenanced and publick virtue becomes the ridicule of the fycophant—when every man of liberality, firmnefs, and penetration, who cannot lick the hand ftretched out to opprefs, is deemed an enemy to the State—then is the gulph of defpotifm fet open, and the grades to flavery, though rapid, are fcarce perceptible—then genius drags heavily its iron chain—fcience is neglefted, and real merit flies to the fhades for fecurity from reproach—the mind becomes enervated, and the national charafter finks to a kind of apathy with only energy fufficient to curfe the breaft that gave it milk, and as an elegant writer obferves, " To bewail " every new birth as an encreafe of mifery, under a govern-" ment where the mind is neceffarily debafed, and talents are " feduced to become the panegyrifts of ufurpation and tyranny." He adds, " that even fedition is not the moft indubitable ene-" my to the publick welfare ; but that its moft dreadful foe is " defpotifm, which always changes the charafter of nations for " the worfe, and is produftive of nothing but vice, that the " tyrant no longer excites to the purfuits of glory or virtue ; " it is not talents,it is bafenefs and fervility that he cherifhes, " and the weight of arbitrary power deftroys the fpring of " emulation."* If fuch is the influence of government on the charafter and manners, and undoubtedly the obfervation is juft, muft we not fubfcribe to the opinion of the celebrated *Abbé Mablé ?* " That there are difagreeable feafons in the un-" happy fituation of human affairs, when policy requires both " the intention and the power of doing mifchief to be punifh-" ed ; and that when the fenate proſcribed the memory of " *Cæfar* they ought to have put *Anthony* to death, and extin-" guifhed the hopes of *Octavius*." Self defence is a primary law of nature, which no fubfequent law of fociety can abolifh ; this primœval principle, the immediate gift of the Creator, obliges every one to remonftrate againft the ftrides of ambition, and a wanton luft of domination, and to refift the firft approaches of tyranny, which at this day threaten to fweep away the rights for which the brave fons of America have fought with an heroifm fcarcely paralleled even in ancient republicks.

It

* HELVITIUS.

It may be repeated, they have purchafed it with their blood,
and have gloried in their independence with a dignity of fpirit,
which has made them the admiration of philofophy, the pride
of America, and the wonder of Europe. It has been obferved,
with great propriety, that " the virtues and vices of a people
" when a revolution happens in their government, are the
".meafure of the liberty or flavery they ought to expect—An
" heroic love for the publick good, a profound reverence for
" the laws, a contempt of riches, and a noble haughtinefs of
" foul, are the only foundations of a free government."* Do
not their dignified principles ftill exift among us ? Or are
they extinguifhed in the breafts of Americans, whofe fields
have been fo recently crimfoned to repel the potent arm of a
foreign Monarch, who had planted his engines of flavery in
every city, with defign to erafe the veftiges of freedom in this
his laft afylum. It is yet to be hoped, for the honour of human nature, that no combinations either foreign or domeftick
have thus darkned this Weftern hemifphere.—On thefe fhores
freedom has planted her ftandard, diped in the purple tide that
flowed from the veins of her martyred heroes ; and here every
uncorrupted American yet hopes to fee it fupported by the
vigour, the juftice, the wifdom and unanimity of the people,
in fpite of the deep-laid plots, the fecret intrigues, or the bold
effrontery of thofe interefted and avaricious adventurers for
place, who intoxicated with the ideas of diftinction and preferment, have proftrated every worthy principle beneath the
fhrine of ambition. Yet thefe are the men who tell us republicanifm is dwindled into theory—that we are incapable of
enjoying our liberties—and that we muft have a mafter.——
Let us retrofpect the days of our adverfity, and recollect who
were then our friends ; do we find them among the fticklers
for ariftocratick authority ? No, they were generally the fame
men who now wifh to fave us from the diftractions of anarchy
on the one hand, and the jaws of tyranny on the other ; where
then were the clafs who now come forth importunately urging
that our political falvation depends on the adoption of a fyftem
at which freedom fpurns ?—Were not fome of them hidden in
the corners of obfcurity, and others wrapping themfelves in
the bofom of our enemies for fafety ? Some of them were in
the arms of infancy ; and others fpeculating for fortune, by
fporting with public money ; while a few, a very few of them
were

were magnanimoufly defending their country, and raifing a character, which I pray heaven may never be fullied by aiding meafures derogatory to their former exertions. But the revolutions in principle which time produces among mankind, frequently exhibits the moft mortifying inftances of human weaknefs ; and this alone can account for the extraordinary appearance of a few names, once diftinguifhed in the honourable walks of patriotifm, but now found on the lift of the Maffachufetts affent to the ratification of a Conftitution, which, by the undefined meaning of fome parts, and the ambiguities of expreffion in others, is dangeroufly adapted to the purpofes of an immediate *ariftocratic tyranny* ; that from the difficulty, if not impracticability of its operation, muft foon terminate in the moft *uncontrouled defpotifm*.

All writers on government agree, and the feelings of the human mind witnefs the truth of thefe political axioms, that man is born free and poffeffed of certain unalienable rights—that government is inftituted for the protection, fafety, and happinefs of the people, and not for the profit, honour, or private intereft of any man, family, or clafs of men——That the origin of all power is in the people, and that they have an inconteftible right to check the creatures of their own creation, vefted with certain powers to guard the life, liberty and property of the community : And if certain felected bodies of men, deputed on thefe principles, determine contrary to the wifhes and expectations of their conftituents, the people have an undoubted right to reject their decifions, to call for a revifion of their conduct, to depute others in their room, or if they think proper, to demand further time for deliberation on matters of the greateft moment : it therefore is an unwarrantable ftretch of authority or influence, if any methods are taken to preclude this reafonable, and peaceful mode of enquiry and decifion. And it is with inexpreffible anxiety, that many of the beft friends to the Union of the States—to the peaceable and equal participation of the rights of nature, and to the glory and dignity of this country, behold the infiduous arts, and the ftrenuous efforts of the partifans of arbitrary power, by their vague definitions of the beft eftablifhed truths, endeavoring to envelope the mind in darknefs the concomitant of flavery, and to lock the ftrong chains of domeftic defpotifm on a country, which by the moft glorious and fuccefsful ftruggles is but newly emancipated from the fceptre of foreign dominion.——

But

But there are certain feafons in the courfe of human affairs,
when Genius, Virtue, and Patriotifm, feems to nod over the
vices of the times, and perhaps never more remarkably, than
at the prefent period ; or we fhould not fee fuch a paffive difpofition prevail in fome, who we muft candidly fuppofe, have
liberal and enlarged fentiments ; while a fupple multitude are
paying a blind and idolatrous homage to the opinions of thofe
who by the moft precipitate fteps are treading down their dear
bought privileges ; and who are endeavouring by all the arts
of infinuation, and influence, to betray the people of the United
States, into an acceptance of a moft complicated fyftem of government ; marked on the one fide with the *dark, fecret* and
profound intrigues, of the ftatefman, long practifed in the pur-
lieus of defpotifm ; and on the other, with the ideal projects of
young ambition, with its wings juft expanded to foar to a fum-
mit, which imagination has painted in fuch gawdy colours as
to intoxicate the *inexperienced votary*, and fend *him* rambling
from State to State, to collect materials to conftruct the ladder
of preferment.

But as a variety of objections to the *heterogeneous phantom*,
have been repeatedly laid before the public, by men of the
beft abilities and intentions ; I will not expatiate long on a
Republican *form* of government, founded on the principles of
monarchy—a democratick branch with the *features* of ariftocracy—and the extravagance of nobility pervading the minds
of many of the candidates for office, with the poverty of pea-
fantry hanging heavily on them, and infurmountable, from
their tafte for expence, unlefs a generous provifion fhould be
made in the arrangement of the civil lift, which may enable
them with the champions of their caufe to " *fail down the new
pactolean channel*." Some gentlemen with laboured zeal, have
fpent much time in urging the neceffity of government, from
the embarraffments of trade—the want of refpectability abroad
and confidence in the public engagements at home :—Thefe
are obvious truths which no one denies ; and there are few
who do not unite in the general wifh for the reftoration of public faith, the revival of commerce, arts, agriculture, and induftry, under a lenient, peaceable and energetick government :
But the moft fagacious advocates for the party have not by fair
difcufion, and rational argumentation, evinced the neceffity of
adopting this many-headed monfter ; of fuch motley mixture,
that its enemies cannot trace a feature of Democratick or Republican

publican extract ; nor have its friends the courage to denomi-
nate it a Monarchy, an Ariftocracy, or an Oligarchy, and the
favoured bantling muft have paffed through the fhort period of
its exiftence without a name, had not Mr. *Wilfon*, in the ferti-
lity of his genius, fuggefted the happy epithet of a *Federal
Republic*.—But I leave the field of general cenfure on the fecrecy of its birth, the rapidity of its growth, and the fatal confequences of fuffering it to live to the age of maturity, and
will particularize fome of the moft weighty objections to its
paffing through this continent in a gigantic fize.—It will be
allowed by every one that the fundamental principle of a free
government, is the equal reprefentation of a free people——
And I will *firft* obferve with a juftly celebrated writer, " That
" the principal aim of fociety is to protect individuals in the
" abfolute rights which were vefted in them by the immediate
" laws of nature, but which could not be preferved in peace,
" without the mutual intercourfe which is gained by the infti-
" tution of friendly and focial communities." And when fociety has thus deputed a certain number of their equals to take
care of their perfonal rights, and the intereft of the whole community, it muft be confidered that refponfibility is the great
fecurity of integrity and honour ; and that annual election is
the bafis of refponfibility.—Man is not immediately corrupted,
but power without limitation, or amenability, may endanger
the brighteft virtue—whereas a frequent return to the bar of
their Conftituents is the ftrongeft check againft the corruptions
to which men are liable, either from the intrigues of others of
more fubtle genius, or the propenfities of their own hearts,—
and the gentlemen who have fo warmly advocated in the late
Convention of the Maffachufetts, the change from annual to
biennial elections ; may have been in the fame predicament,
and perhaps with the fame views that Mr. *Hutchinfon* once acknowledged himfelf, when in a letter to *Lord Hillfborough*, he
obferved, " that the grand difficulty of making a change in
" government againft the general bent of the people had caufed
" him to turn his thoughts to a variety of plans, in order to
" find one that might be executed in fpite of oppofition," and
the firft he propofed was that, " inftead of annual, the elections
" fhould be only once in three years :" but the Minifter had
not the hardinefs to attempt fuch an innovation, even in the
revifion of colonial charters : nor has any one ever defended
Beiunial, Triennial, or Septennial, Elections, either in the
Britifh

Britifh Houfe of Commons, or in the debates of Provincial
affemblies, on general and free principles : but it is unneceffary
to dwell long on this article, as the beft political writers have
fupported the principles of annual elections with a precifion,
that cannot be confuted, though they may be darkned, by the
fophiftical arguments that have been thrown out with defign,
to undermine all the barriers of freedom.

2. There is no fecurity in the profered fyftem, either for
the rights of confcience, or the liberty of the Prefs : Defpotifm
ufually while it is gaining ground, will fuffer men to think,
fay, or write what they pleafe ; but when once eftablifhed, if
it is thought neceffary to fubferve the purpofes of arbitrary
power, the moft unjuft reftrictions may take place in the firft
inftance,and an *imprimator* on thePrefs in the next, may filence
the complaints, and forbid the moft decent remonftrances of
an injured and oppreffed people.

3. There are no well defined limits of the Judiciary Powers,
they feem to be left as a boundlefs ocean, that has broken over
the chart of the Supreme Lawgiver " *thus far fhalt thou go and
no further,*" and as they cannot be comprehended by the clear-
eft capacity, or the moft fagacious mind, it would be an Her-
culean labour to attempt to defcribe the dangers with which
they are replete.

4. The Executive and the Legiflative are fo dangeroufly
blended as to give juft caufe of alarm, and every thing relative
thereto, is couched in fuch ambiguous terms—in fuch vague
and indifinite expreffion, as is a fufficient ground without any
other objection, for the reprobation of a fyftem, that the authors
dare not hazard to a clear inveftigation.

5. The abolition of trial by jury in civil caufes.—This mode
of trial the learned Judge Blackftone obferves, " has been co-
" eval with the firft rudiments of civil government, that pro-
" perty, liberty and life, depend on maintaining in its legal
" force the conftitutional trial by jury." He bids his readers
pauze, and with Sir Matthew Hale obferves, how admirably
this mode is adapted to the inveftigation of truth beyond any
other the world can produce. Even the party who have been
difpofed to fwallow, without examination, the propofals of the
fecret conclave, have ftarted on a difcovery that this effential
right was curtailed ; and fhall a privilege, the origin of which
may be traced to our Saxon anceftors—that has been a part of
the law of nations, even in the fewdatory fyftems of France,
Germany

Germany and Italy—and from the earlieft records has been
held fo facred, both in ancient and modern Britain, that it
could never be fhaken by the introduction of Norman cuftoms,
or any other conquefts or change of government——fhall this
ineftimable privilege be relinquifhed in America—either thro'
the fear of inquifition for unaccounted thoufands of public
monies in the hands of fome who have been officious in the
fabrication of the *confolidated fyftem*, or from the apprehenfion
that fome future delinquent poffeffed of more power than integrity, may be called to a trial by his peers in the hour of inveftigation ?

6. Though it has been faid by Mr. *Wilfon* and many others,
that a Standing-Army is neceffary for the dignity and fafety
of America, yet freedom revolts at the idea, when the Divan,
or the Defpot, may draw out his dragoons to fupprefs the
murmurs of a few, who may yet cherifh thofe fublime principles which call forth the exertions, and lead to the beft improvement of the human mind. It is hoped this country may
yet be governed by milder methods than are ufually difplayed
beneath the bannerets of military law.—Standing armies have
been the nurfery of vice and the bane of liberty from the Roman legions, to the eftablifhment of the artful Ximenes, and
from the ruin of the Cortes of Spain, to the planting the Britifh cohorts in the capitals of America :—By the edicts of authority vefted in the fovereign power by the propofed conftitution, the militia of the country, the bulwark of defence, and
the fecurity of national liberty is no longer under the controul
of civil authority ; but at the refcript of the Monarch, or the
ariftocracy, they may either be employed to extort the enor-
mous fums that will be neceffary to fupport the civil lift—to
maintain the regalia of power—and the fplendour of the moft
ufelefs part of the community, or they may be fent into foreign
countries for the fulfilment of treaties, ftipulated by the Prefident and two thirds of the Senate.

7. Notwithftanding the delufory promifs to guarantee a
Republican form of government to every State in the Union—
If the moft difcerning eye could difcover any meaning at all in
the engagement, there are no refources left for the fupport
of internal government, or the liquidation of the debts of the
State. Every fource of revenue is in the monopoly of Congrefs,
and if the feveral legiflatures in their enfeebled ftate, fhould a-
gainft their own feelings be neceffitated to attempt a dry tax
for

for the payment of their debts, and the support of internal
police, even this may be required for the purposes of the general government.

8. As the new Congress are empowered to determine their
own salaries, the requisitions for this purpose may not be very
moderate, and the drain for public moneys will probably rise
past all calculation : and it is to be feared when America has
consolidated its despotism, the world will witness the truth of
the assertion —" that the pomp of an eastern monarch may
" impose on the vulgar who may estimate the force of a nation
" by the magnificence of its palaces ; but the wise man, judges
" differently, it is by that very magnificence he estimates its
" weakness. He sees nothing more in the midst of this impos-
" ing pomp, where the tyrant sets enthroned, than a sumptu-
" ous and mournful decoration of the dead ; the apparatus of a
" fastuous funeral, in the centre of which is a cold and lifeless
" lump of unanimated earth, a phantom of power ready to
" disappear before the enemy, by whom it is despised !"

9. There is no provision for a rotation, nor any thing to
prevent the perpetuity of office in the some hands for life ;
which by a little well timed bribery, will probably be done,
to the exclusion of men of the best abilities from their share in
the offices of government.—By this neglect we lose the advantages of that check to the overbearing insolence of office, which
by rendering him ineligible at certain periods, keeps the mind
of man in equilibrio, and teaches him the feelings of the governed, and better qualifies him to govern in his turn.

10. The inhabitants of the United States, are liable to be
draged from the vicinity of their own county, or state, to answer to the litigious or unjust suit of an adversary, on the most
distant borders of the Continent : in short the appelate jurisdiction of the Supreme Federal Court, includes an unwarrantable stretch of power over the liberty, life, and property of
the subject, through the wide Continent of America.

11. One Representative to thirty thousand inhabitants is a
very inadequate representation ; and every man who is not
lost to all sense of freedom to his country, must reprobate the
idea of Congress altering by law, or on any pretence whatever, interfering with any regulations for the time, places, and
manner of choosing our own Representatives.

12. If the sovereignty of America is designed to be elective,
the circumscribing the votes to only ten electors in this State,

B   and

and the fame proportion in all the others, is nearly tantamount to the exclufion of the voice of the people in the choice of their firft inagiftrate. It is vefting the choice folely in an ariftocratic junto, who may eafily combine in each State to place at the head of the Union the moft convenient inftrument for defpotic fway.

13. A Senate chofen for fix years will, in moft inftances, be an appointment for life, as the influence of fuch a body over the minds of the people will be coequal to the extenfive powers with which they are vefted, and they will not only forget, but be forgotten by their conftituents—a branch of the Supreme Legiflature thus fet beyond all refponfibility is totally repugnant to every principle of a free government.

14. There is no provifion by a bill of rights to guard againft the dangerous encroachments of power in too many inftances to be named : but I cannot pafs over in filence the infecurity in which we are left with regard to warrants unfupported by evidence—the daring experiment of granting *writs of affiftance* in a former arbitrary adminiftration is not yet forgotten in the Maffachufetts ; nor can we be fo ungrateful to the memory of the patriots who counteraded their operation, as fo foon after their manly exertions to fave us from fuch a deteftable inftrument of arbitrary power, to fubjed ourfelves to the infolence of any petty revenue officer to enter our houfes, fearch, infult,and feize at pleafure. We are told by a gentleman of too much virtue and real probity to fufped he has a defign to deceive—" that the whole conftitution is a declaration of rights" —but mankind muft think for themfelves, and to many very judicious and difcerning characters, the whole conftitution with very few exceptions appears a perverfion of the rights of particular ftates, and of private citizens.——But the gentleman goes on to tell us, " that the primary objed is the general go- " vernment, and that the rights of individuals are only inci- " dentally mentioned, and that there was a clear impropriety " in being very particular about them." But, afking pardon for diffenting from fuch refpedable authority, who has been led into feveral miftakes, more from his predilidion in favour of certain modes of government, than from a want of underftanding or veracity. The rights of individuals ought to be the primary objed of all government, and cannot be too fecurely guarded by the moft explicit declarations in their favor. This has been the opinion of the Hampdens, the Pyms, and many

many other illuftrious names, that have ftood forth in defence
of Englifh liberties ; and even the Italian mafter in politicks,
the fubtle and renouned Machiavel acknowledges, that no republic ever yet ftood on a ftable foundation without fatisfying
the common people.

15. The difficulty, if not impracticability, of exercifing the
equal and equitable powers of government by a fingle legiflature over an extent of territory that reaches from the Miffifippi
to the Weftern lakes, and from them to the Atlantic ocean, is
an infuperable objection to the adoption of the new fyftem.—
Mr. *Hutchinfon*, the great champion for arbitrary power, in the
multitude of his machinations to fubvert the liberties of this
ccuntry, was obliged to acknowledge in one of his letters, that,
" from the extent of country from north to fouth, the fcheme
" of one government was impracticable." But if the authors
of the prefent vifionary project, can by the arts of deception,
precipitation and addrefs, obtain a majority of fuffrages in the
conventions of the ftates to try the hazardous experiment, they
may then make the fame inglorious boaft with this infidious
politician, who may perhaps be their model, that " the union
" of the colonies was pretty well broken, and that he hoped
" never to fee it revewed."

16. It is an indifputed fact, that not one legiflature in the
United States had the moft diftant idea when they firft appointed members for a convention, entirely commercial, or when
they afterwards authorifed them to confider on fome amendments of the Federal union, that they would without any war-
rant from their conftituents, prefume on fo bold and daring a
ftride, as ultimately to deftroy the ftate governments, and
offer a *confolidated fyftem*, irreverfible but on conditions that
the fmalleft degree of penetration muft difcover to be impracticable.

17. The firft appearance of the article which declares the
ratification of nine ftates fufficient for the eftablifhment of the
new fyftem, wears the face of diffention, is a fubverfion of the
union of the Confederated States, and tends to the introduction
of anarchy and civil convulfions, and may be a means of in-
volving the whole country in blood.

18. The mode in which this conftitution is recommended
to the people to judge without either the advice of Congrefs,
or the legiflatures of the feveral ftates, is very reprehenfible—
it is an attempt to force it upon them before it could be tho-
roughly

roughly underſtood, and may leave us in that ſituation, that in the firſt moments of ſlavery the minds of the people agitated by the remembrance of their loſt liberties, will be like the ſea in a tempeſt, that ſweeps down every mound of ſecurity.

But it is needleſs to enumerate other inſtances, in which the propoſed conſtitution appears contradictory to the firſt principles which ought to govern mankind ; and it is equally ſo to enquire into the motives that induced to ſo bold a ſtep as the annihilation of the independence and ſovereignty of the thirten diſtinct ſtates.——They are but too obvious through the whole progreſs of the buſineſs, from the firſt ſhutting up the doors of the federal convention and reſolving that no member ſhould correſpond with gentlemen in the different ſtates on the ſubject under diſcuſſion ; till the trivial propoſition of *recommending* a few amendments was artfully uſhered into the convention of the Maſſachuſetts. The queſtions that were then before that honorable-aſſembly were profound and important, they were of ſuch magnitude and extent, that the conſequences may run parallel with the exiſtence of the country ; and to ſee them waved and haſtily terminated by a meaſure too abſurd to require a ſerious refutation, raiſes the honeſt indignation of every true lover of his country. Nor are they leſs grieved that the ill policy and arbitrary diſpoſition of ſome of the ſons of America has thus precipitated to the contemplation and diſcuſion of queſtions that no one could rationally ſuppoſe would have been agitated among us, till time had blotted out the principles on which the late revolution was grounded ; or till the laſt traits of the many political tracts, which defended the ſeperation from Britain, and the rights of men were conſigned to everlaſting oblivion. After the ſevere conflicts this country has ſuffered, it is preſumed that they are diſpoſed to make every reaſonable ſacrifice before the altar of peace.—— But when we contemplate the nature of men and conſider them originally on an equal footing, ſubject to the ſame feelings, ſtimulated by the ſame paſſions, and recollecting the ſtruggles they have recently made, for the ſecurity of their civil rights ; it cannot be expected that the inhabitants of the Maſſachuſetts, can be eaſily lulled into a fatal ſecurity, by the declamatory effuſions of gentlemen, who, contrary to the experience of all ages would perſwade them there is no danger to be apprehended, from veſting diſcretionary powers in the hands of man, which he may, or may not abuſe. The very ſuggeſtion, that

we

we ought to truſt to the precarious hope of amendments and redreſs, after we have voluntarily fixed the ſhackles on our own necks ſhould have awakened to a double degree of caution.—This people have not forgotten the artful inſinuations of a former Governor, when pleading the unlimited authority of parliament before the legiſlature of the Maſſachuſetts ; nor that his arguments were very ſimilar to ſome lately urged by gentlemen who boaſt of oppoſing his meaſures, " *with halters about their necks.*"

We were then told by him, in all the ſoft language of inſinuation, that no form of government of human conſtruction can be perfect—that we had nothing to fear—that we had no reaſon to complain—that we had only to acquieſce in their illegal claims, and to ſubmit to the requiſitions of parliament, and doubtleſs the lenient hand of government would redreſs all grievances, and remove the oppreſſions of the people :—Yet we ſoon ſaw armies of mercenaries encamped on our plains —our commerce ruined—our harbours blockaded—and our cities burnt. It may be replied, that this was in conſequence of an obſtinate defence of our privileges ; this may be true ; and when the " *ultima ratic*" is called to aid, the weakeſt muſt fall. But let the beſt informed hiſtorian produce an inſtance when bodies of men were intruſted with power, and the proper checks relinquiſhed, if they were ever found deſtitute of ingenuity ſufficient to furniſh pretences to abuſe it. And the people at large are already ſenſible, that the liberties which America has claimed, which reaſon has juſtified, and which have been ſo glorioũſly defended by the ſword of the brave ; are not about to fall before the tyranny of foreign conqueſt : it is native uſurpation that is ſhaking the foundations of peace, and ſpreading the ſable curtain of deſpotiſm over the United States. The banners of freedom were erected in the wilds of America by our anceſtors, while the wolf prowled for his prey on the one hand, and more ſavage man on the other ; they have been ſince reſcued from the invading hand of foreign power, by the valor and blood of their poſterity ; and there was reaſon to hope they would continue for ages to illumine a quarter of the globe, by nature kindly ſeperated from the proud monarchies of Europe, and the infernal darkneſs of Aſiatic ſlavery.——And it is to be feared we ſhall ſoon ſee this country ruſhing into the extremes of confuſion and violence, in conſequence of the proceedings of a ſet of gentlemen, who diſregard-

ing

ing the purpofes of their appointment, have affumed powers
unauthorifed by any commiffion, have unneceffarily rejected the
confederation of the United States, and annihilated the fovereignty and independence of the individual governments.—
The caufes which have infpired a few men affembled for very
different purpofes with fuch a degree of temerity us to break
with a fingle ftroke the union of America, and diffeminate
the feeds of difcord through the land may be eafily inveftigat-
ed, when we furvey the patizans of monarchy in the ftate conventions, urging the adoption of a mode of government that
militates with the former profeffions and exertions of this
country, and with all ideas of republicanifm, and the equal
rights of men.

Paffion, prejudice, and error, are characteriftics of human
nature ; and as it cannot be accounted for on any principles of
philofophy, religion, or good policy ; to thefe fhades in the
human character muft be attributed the mad zeal of fome, to
precipitate to a blind adoption of the meafures of the late federal convention, without giving opportunity for better information to thofe who are mifled by influence or ignorance into
erroneous opinions.——Litterary talents may be proftituted,
and the powers of genius debafed to fubferve the purpofes of
ambition, or avarice ; but the feelings of the heart will dictate
the language of truth, and the fimplicity of her accents will
proclaim the infamy of thofe, who betray the rights of the
people, under the fpecious, and popular pretence of *juftice,
confolidation*, and *dignity*.

It is prefumed the great body of the people unite in fenti-
ment with the writer of thefe obfervations, who moft devoutly
prays that public credit may rear her declining head, and re-
munerative juftice pervade the land ; nor is there a doubt if a
free government is continued, that time and induftry will enable both the public and private debtor to liquidate their ar-
rearages in the moft equitable manner. They wifh to fee the
Confederated States bound together by the moft indiffolub e
union, but without renouncing their feperate fovereignties and
independence, and becoming tributaries to a confolidated fa-
brick of ariftocratick tyranny.————They wifh to fee
government eftablifhed, and peaceably holding the reins with
honour, energy, and dignity ; but they wifh for no *federal
city* whofe " *cloud cap't towers*" may fcreen the ftate culprit
from the hand of juftice ; while its exclufive jurifdiction may
protect

protect the riot of armies encamped within its limits.---They deprecate difcord and civil convulfions, but they are not yet generally prepared with the ungrateful Ifraelites to afk a King, nor are their fpirits fufficiently broken to yield the beft of their olive grounds to his fervants, and to fee their fons appointed to run before his chariots—It has been obferved by a zealous advocate for the new fyftem, that moft governments are the refult of fraud or violence, and this with defign to recommend its acceptance—but has not almoft every ftep towards its fabrication been fraudulent in the extreme ? Did not the prohibition ftrictly enjoined by the general Convention, that no member fhould make any communication to his Conftituents, or to gentlemen of confideration and abilities in the other States, bear evident marks of fraudulent defigns ?—This circumftance is regretted in ftrong terms by Mr. Martin, a member from Maryland, who acknowledges " He had no idea that all the " wifdom, integrity, and virtue of the States was contained in " that Convention, and that he wifhed to have correfponded " with gentlemen of eminent political characters abroad, and " to give their fentiments due weight"—he adds, "; fo ex- " tremely folicitous were they, that their proceedings fhould " not tranfpire, that the members were prohibited from taking " copies of their refolutions, or extracts from the Journals, " without exprefs permiffion, by vote."——And the hurry with which it has been urged to the acceptance of the people, without giving time, by adjournments, for better information, and more unanimity has a deceptive appearance ; and if finally driven to refiftance, as the only alternative between that and fervitude, till in the confufion of difcord, the reins fhould be feized by the violence of fome enterprizing genius, that may fweep down the laft barrier of liberty, it muft be added to the fcore of criminality with which the fraudulent ufurpation at Philadelphia, may be chargeable.——Heaven avert fuch a tremendous fcence ! and let us ftill hope a more happy termination of the prefent ferment :—may the people be calm, and wait a legal redrefs ; may the mad tranfport of fome of our infatuated capitals fubfide ; and every influential character through the States, make the moft prudent exertions for a new general Convention, who may veft adequate powers in Congrefs, for all national purpofes, without annihilating the individual governments, and drawing blood from every pore by taxes, impofitions and illegal reftrictions.—This ftep might

again

again re-eftablifh the Union, reftore} ranquility to the ruffled mind of the inhabitants, and fave America from diftreffes, dreadful even in contemplation.———" The great art of governing is to lay afide all prejudices and attachments to particular opinions, claffes or individual characters ; to confult the fpirit of the people ; to give way to it ; and in fo doing, to give it a turn capable of infpiring thofe fentiments, which may induce them to relifh a change, which an alteration of circumftances may hereafter make neceffary."———The education of the advocates for monarchy fhould have taught them, and their memory fhould have fuggefted that " monarchy is a fpecies of government fit only for a people too much corrupted by luxury, avarice, and a paffion for pleafure, to have any love for their country, and whofe vices the fear of punifhment alone is able to reftrain ; but by no means calculated for a nation that is poor, and at the fame time tenacious of their liberty—animated with a difguft to tyranny—and infpired with the generous feelings of patriotifm and liberty, and at the fame time, like the anicient Spartans have been hardened by temperance and manly exertions, and equally defpifing the fatigues of the field, and the fear of enemies,"———and while they change their ground they fhould recollect, that Ariftocracy is ftill a more formidable foe to public virtue, and the profperity of a nation—that under fuch a government her patriots become mercenaries—her foldiers, cowards, and the people flaves.———Though feveral State Conventions have affented to, and ratified, yet the voice of the people appears at prefent ftrong againft the adoption of 'the Conftitution.———By the chicanery, intrigue, and falfe colouring of thofe who plume themfelves, more on their education and abilities, than their political, patriotic, or private virtues —by the imbecility of fome, and the duplicity of others, a majority of theConvention of Maffachufetts have been flattered with the ideas of amendments, when it will be too late to complain———While feveral very worthy characters, too timid for their fituation, magnified the hopelefs alternative, between the diffolution of the bands of all government, and receiving the proffered fyftem *in toto*, after long endeavouring to reconcile it to their confciences, fwallowed the indigeftible penacea, and in a kind of fudden defperation lent their fignature to the dereliction of the honorable ftation they held in the Union, and have broken over the folemn compact, by which they were bound to fupport their own excellent conftitution till the period

of

of revifion.—Yet Virginia, equally large and refpectable, and who have done honour to themfelves, by their vigorous exertions from the firft dawn of independence, have not yet acted upon the queftion ; they have wifely taken time to confider before they introduce innovations of a moft dangerous nature : ——her inhabitants are brave, her burgeffes are free, and they have a Governor who dares to think for himfelf, and to fpeak his opinion (without firft pouring libations on the altar of popularity) though it fhould militate with fome of the moft accomplifhed and illuftrious characters.

Maryland, who has no local intereft to lead her to adopt, will doubtlefs reject the fyftem——I hope the fame characters ftill live, and that the fame fpirit which dictated to them a wife and cautious care, againft fudden revolutions in government, and made them the laft State that acceded to the independence of America, will lead them to fupport what they fo deliberately claimed.——Georgia apprehenfive of a war with the Savages, has acceded in order to infure protection.——Pennfylvania has ftruggled through much in the fame manner, as the Maffachufetts, againft the manly feelings, and the mafterly reafonings of a very refpectable part of the Convention . They have adopted the fyftem, and feen fome of its authors burnt in effigy—their towns thrown into riot and confufion, and the minds of the people agitated by apprehenfion and difcord.

New-Jerfey and Delaware have united in the meafure, from the locality of their fituation, and the felfifh motives which too generally govern mankind ; the Federal City, and the feat of government, will naturally attract the intercourfe of ftrangers—the youth of enterprize, and the wealth of the nation to the central States.

Connecticut has pufhed it through with the precipitation of her neighbour, with few diffentient voices ;—but more from irritation and refentment to a fifter State, perhaps partiality to herfelf in her commercial regulations, than from a comprehenfive view of the fyftem, as a regard to the welfare of all.——But New-York has motives, that will undoubtedly lead her to a rejection, without being afraid to appeal to the underftanding of mankind, to juftify the grounds of their refufal to adopt a Conftitution, that even the framers dare not rifque to the hazard of revifion, amendment, or reconfideration, leaft the whole fuperftructure fhould be demolifhed by more fkilful and difcreet architects,——I know not what part the Carolinas

C will

will take ; but I hope their determinations will comport with the dignity and freedom of this country—their decisions will have great weight in the scale.————But equally important are the small States of New-Hampshire and Rhode-Island :—New-York, the Carolinas, Virginia, Maryland, and these two lesser States may yet support the liberties of the Continent ; if they refuse a ratification, or postpone their proceedings till the spirits of the community have time to cool, there is little doubt but the wise measure of another federal convention will be adopted, when the members would have the advantage of viewing, at large, through the medium of truth, the objections that have been made from various quarters ; such a measure might be attended with the most salutary effects, and prevent the dread consequences of civil feuds.————But even if some of those large states should hastily accede, yet we have frequently seen in the story of revolution, relief spring from a quarter least expected.

Though the virtues of a Cato could not save Rome, nor the abilities of a Padilla defend the citizens of Castile from falling under the yoke of Charles ; yet a *Tell* once suddenly rose from a little obscure city, and boldly rescued the liberties of his country.————Every age has its Bruti and its Decii, as well as its Cæsars and Sejani :—The happiness of mankind depends much on the modes of government, and the virtues of the governors ; and America may yet produce characters who have genius and capacity sufficient to form the manners and correct the morals of the people, and virtue enough to lead their country to freedom.   Since her dismemberment from the British empire, America has, in many instances, resembled the conduct of a restless, vigorous, luxurious youth, prematurely emancipated from the authority of a parent, but without the experience necessary to direct him to act with dignity or discretion.   Thus we have seen her break the shackles of foreign dominion, and all the blessings of peace restored on the most honourable terms : She acquired the liberty of framing her own laws, choosing her own magistrates, and adopting manners and modes of government the most favourable to the freedom and happiness of society.   But how little have we availed ourselves of these superior advantages : The glorious fabric of liberty successfully reared with so much labour and assiduity totters to the foundation, and may be blown away as the bubble of fancy by the rude breath of military combinations, and politicians of yesterday.

It is true this country lately armed in opposition to regal despotism—impoverished by the expences of a long war, and unable immediately to fulfil their public or private engagements, have appeared in some instances, with a boldness of spirit that seemed to set at defiance all authority, government, or order, on the one hand ; while on the other, there has been, not only a secret wish, but an open avowal of the necessity of drawing the reins of government much too taught, not only for republicanism, but for a wise and limited monarchy.——— But the character of this people is not averse to a degree of subordination : the truth of this appears from the easy restoration of tranquility, after a dangerous insurrection in one of the states ; this also evinces the little necessity of a complete revolution of government throughout the union. But it is a republican principle that the majority should rule ; and if a spirit of moderation could be cultivated on both sides, till the voice of the people at large could be fairly heard it should be held sacred - And if, on such a scrutiny, the proposed constitution should appear repugnant to their character and wishes ; if they, in the language of a late elegant pen, should acknowledge that " no confusion in my mind, is more terrible to them " than the stern disciplined regularity and vaunted police of " arbitrary governments, where every heart is depraved by " fear, where mankind dare not assume their natural characters, " where the free spirit must crouch to the slave in office, where " genius must repress her effusions, or like the Egyptian wor- " shippers, offer them in sacrifice to the calves in power, and " where the human mind, always in shackles, shrinks from " every generous effort." Who would then have the effrontory to say, it ought not to be thrown out with indignation, however some respectable names have appeared to support it.——— But if after all, on a dispassionate and fair discussion, the people generally give their voice for a voluntary dereliction of their privileges, let every individual who chooses the active scenes of life, strive to support the peace and unanimity of his country, though every other blessing may expire—And while the statesman is plodding for power, and the courtier practising the arts of dissimulation without check—while the rapacious are growing rich by oppression, and fortune throwing her gifts into the lap of fools, let the sublimer characters, the philosophic lovers of freedom who have wept over her exit, retire to the calm shades of contemplation, there they may look down with pity on the inconsistency of human nature, the revolutions of states, the rise of kingdoms, and the fall of empires.